D1611967

SHORT STORIES OF YASHPAL

YASHPAL

SHORT
STORIES
OF
YASHPAL
AUTHOR AND PATRIOT

Translated and Introduced by

Corinne Friend

UNIVERSITY OF PENNSYLVANIA PRESS
Philadelphia

Copyright © 1969 by
The Trustees of the University of Pennsylvania

Library of Congress Catalog Card Number 78–87939
Printed in the United States of America
SBN: 8122–7601–9

For Irwin

CONTENTS

AUTHOR'S NOTE

This volume of stories grew out of my graduate program in the South Asia Regional Studies Department of the University of Pennsylvania. I owe a profound debt of gratitude to Ernest Bender, Professor of Indo-Aryan Languages and Literatures, for encouragement and help unstintingly given in supervising my study. I was the beneficiary of his generosity in sharing his vast and intimate knowledge of the language, the literature and the country we studied. Six of the nine short stories which appear here were translated under his supervision. Later, for this volume, I translated the other three: "To Uphold Righteousness," "One Cigarette," and "The Book of Experience."

To W. Norman Brown, Emeritus Professor of Sanskrit, my special thanks for making freely available his great gifts of scholarship and for innumerable boons so graciously given that I almost felt that I had earned them as a right.

To R. L. Agarwal, who read Hindi with me, I owe the appreciation earned by one who opens a window to a wider world. He was my interpreter of the Indian scene, my companion and sharer of many afternoons in the beautiful Indian winter sun, where we read and drank tea and had talks which enriched my understanding of everything I saw.

To Yashpal and his firm, Viplav Karyalay of Lucknow, publisher of these stories in the original Hindi, I express my

appreciation for permission to publish the English translations. My translations of "Sāg" and "The Emperor's Justice," which first appeared in *Mahfil,* Autumn, 1967, issue,
are reprinted with permission.

Corinne Friend

Wynnewood, Pennsylvania
June, 1969

NOTE ON TRANSLATION
AND PRONUNCIATION

Some arbitrary decisions had to be made concerning diacritical markings. In general, words and books that are well known in English are treated as English words. All proper names are also shown without diacritical markings.

In the story "To Uphold Righteousness," however, although a large number of words may not be known to the average reader, I avoided diacritical markings to a greater extent than in other stories because I felt that too high a proportion of words so marked would be distracting. These words are, of course, explained in footnotes.

Some inconsistencies in spelling should be pointed out. Both "Brahman" and "Brahmin" appear as alternate spellings; qazi is also shown as kazi; Dayanand is sometimes Dayananda, etc. One of the problems of transliteration from Devanagari script is the absence of standard practice. Where quoting from other sources, I have been bound by the author's spelling.

For those words shown in the text with diacritical markings, and therefore transliterated from Hindi or Sanskrit, a rough guide to pronunciation is as follows: The vowel sounds *a, ā, i, ī, u, ū, e, ai, o, au* are pronounced as in the English words *us, far, big, fleet, put, boot, make, buy, no, now,* respectively. The consonant *c* is pronounced *ch* as in *chip; g* is *g* as in *gap; ṣ* is *sh* as in *shop.* The sounds *ṭ, ḍ,* and *ṇ* are made with the tongue against the back of the teeth; *ṭ, ḍ,* and *ṇ* are made with the tip of the tongue turned up and drawn farther back into the dome of the palate. The aspirate sounds *th, kh, ph,* resemble the sounds of *t, k, p,* as in *tip, kid, pin*— that is, the initial consonant is followed by a puff of breath. The aspirates *dh, gh, bh* are like the combinations in *madhouse, doghouse, clubhouse.*

The next to last syllable is stressed if it is a long syllable. If it is not, the first long syllable before it is stressed. A long syllable is one containing *ā, ī, ū, e, o, ai, au* or a vowel followed by more than one consonant. Usually *h* following a consonant indicates aspiration of the consonant and gives length to the syllable.

INTRODUCTION

YASHPAL, a revolutionary fighting for India's freedom, was twenty-eight years old when he was caught, tried, and sentenced to fourteen years to life at hard labor. There was little expectation at that time that he would emerge as one of India's outstanding writers of fiction.

He has led two lives, and in each of them has made important contributions to his country. His first life was dedicated to her freedom, his present life to her literature.

Ironically, some of India's best known literature has been produced in her prisons. Mahatma Gandhi and Jawaharlal Nehru, in prison cells, wrote movingly of India's right to freedom. We of the Western world were among their beneficiaries, for by writing in English, they shared their feelings with us. However, when Yashpal began to write in prison, he made an important decision—one that affected the size and composition of his future audience, but which was consistent with the character of the man. He decided to write in Hindi. He could as easily have written in English, but the reasons for his choice, in his words, were:

> First I started writing in English. I filled several exercise books. Then I thought, "I have my own language,

3

why don't I write in that language? If I can write
something worthwhile from a literary standpoint, is it
my duty to enrich the literature of English or of my
own language—Hindi?" I was so convinced of the
rightness of this that I made a kind of vow to write
only in Hindi, and I would examine all that I wrote
with the eyes of a hard judge or critic.[1]

Readers of Hindi have indeed gained by Yashpal's decision
and readers of English have correspondingly lost. There
is a need to present to a wider world the best literature
that Indians have written for Indians alone. That is the
reason for these nine stories translated into English as a
sampling of Yashpal.

The short story and novel have become a feature of Hindi
literature only in the last one hundred years. Medieval Hindi
literature was characterized mainly by poetry of three kinds,
each predominating in a different period of time. Earliest
were the poems composed by bards for the court, telling tales
of war and chivalry, praising the king. The middle period saw
the growth of *bhakti* or the devotional movement, which
produced hymns by religious poets for the people, singing
songs of love and devotion to the Lord. Finally, a type of
secular court poetry based on ancient rules of Sanskrit poetics,
and designed to display the virtuosity of the poet, came into
vogue.

Bardic poetry, which flourished in North India from about
the eighth century until the fourteenth, reflected the feudal
conditions of that era. Continual warfare among the petty,
rival Hindu kingdoms made North India easy prey to Muslim

[1] Yashpal, *Sinhāvalokan*, Volume 3, Lucknow: Viplav Karyalay, 1961,
p. 150.

invasion from the north and west. By the end of the fourteenth century Muslim power over North India was consolidated and complete. The results of war, invasion, and then subjection to a foreign ruler with an alien culture turned people's thoughts and emotions inward, and they looked to God for solace and inspiration. Their quest resulted in a great literary and religious movement—*bhakti*.

The two greatest poets of the *bhakti* movement were the saint Kabir, born a Muslim (c. 1440–1518) and the Hindu poet Tulsidas (c. 1532–1623). The hymns of Kabir promoted the blending of Hindu and Muslim cultures by stressing the oneness of God and His love for humanity.[2]

The work of Tulsidas represented a different stream of the *bhakti* movement, one which was purely Hindu in its inspiration. He worshiped God in human form as Rama, and for the literary qualities of his *Ramayana* Tulsidas is considered Hindi's greatest poet.[3]

Referring to Tulsidas, Ainslie Embree has said:

> . . . it would be difficult to overestimate his significance for the religious and moral life of North India.
> . . . Westerners used to say that Tulasidas' work was the Bible of India, but that comparison is inadequate now, for Tulasidas' book is probably better known today in North India than the Bible is in any country in the West.[4]

[2] See *Songs of Kabir,* translated by Rabindranath Tagore, New York: Macmillan, 1915.

[3] See English translations: F. S. Growse, *The Rāmāyaṇa of Tulsī Dās,* Allahabad: North-Western Provinces and Oudh Government Press, 1883. Also W. Douglas Hill, *The Holy Lake of the Acts of Rama,* London: Geoffrey Cumberlege, 1952

[4] Ainslie T. Embree, *The Hindu Tradition,* New York: The Modern Library, 1966, pp. 248–49

By the seventeenth century, a new type of secular court poetry was patronized by the Moghul courts. This literature, composed for the court, adopted the rules of Sanskrit poetics and imitated and elaborated on old forms. Addressing itself to sound-play and word-play it became contrived and narrow. Just as Indian political life was declining, losing its vigor and inspiration, so was Hindi literature. However, by the middle of the nineteenth century, new and revitalizing forces from the West had intruded into India again, resulting in changes both in political life and literature.

The Moghul Empire ended abruptly and dramatically with the suppression of the Indian Mutiny in 1857. British paramountcy was established and steps were taken to centralize the administration of the country. During the nineteenth century, communications by road, railway, and postal and telegraph service were improved. The printing press stimulated journalism and book production. Christian missionaries were helping to develop literature in regional languages and were exercising a socially democratizing influence as well. Universities were established teaching Western literature, thereby stimulating the development of the short story, novel, and essay. The teaching of Western philosophy gave rise to the concepts of nationalism and social reform. All these forces had an especially important influence on the people whose language was Hindi, for these were the people of the Indo-Gangetic plain, which has been the route of invasion from the west since India's earliest history, and has therefore always been susceptible to new ideas. As a result, a vital segment of modern Hindi literature has been characterized by a spirit of nationalism and reform.

Along these lines of development, three of the most important contributors to modern Hindi literature have been Swami Dayanand Saraswati (1824–1883), Prem Chand (1880–1936), and Yashpal (1903–   ).

Swami Dayanand represented one kind of reaction to the impact of Western culture—a total rejection of the West and reaffirmation of Hindu values. However, it was Hinduism with a difference—purified and reformed. He asserted that the Vedas, the holy scriptures of Hinduism, gave no authority for the corruptions which had entered the fabric of Indian life, such as child marriage, sati, subjection of women, untouchability, and idol worship. He denounced the corruption of the priesthood and asserted that knowledge of the Vedas should be available to all. Vedic knowledge had remained exclusive because it had been available only in Sanskrit. Swami Dayanand's valuable contribution to Hindi literature was *Satyārth Prākāsh (The Light of Truth)*, his commentaries in Hindi on the Vedas and the Upanishads.

By contributing to Hindi literature in this way, he brought to the common people a sense of participation and importance. By preaching against social evils and invoking Hindu scripture as authority, he counteracted the claims of the moral superiority of Christianity and the West. By supporting education for girls as well as boys, he was a vital force in raising the status of women. He founded the Arya Samaj as a society for social service and education. The Samaj in turn established colleges which became centers of nationalist activity in northern India.

He referred to a glorious, if largely mythical, Indian past which was free of social and religious evils, and by extension sought an equally glorious future for India by remedying those evils. Although Yashpal rejects the narrow Hindu bias of Swami Dayanand's teaching and his extravagant claims concerning ancient India, nonetheless his own early feelings of Indian nationality and pride were fostered by his education in gurukul, a school founded by a disciple of Swami Dayanand.

Although Swami Dayanand's work did not have great literary merit, it is significant for the course of modern Hindi literature that he chose Hindi over Gujarati, his mother tongue, in order to reach the greatest number of people with his message of nationalism and reform. Later, Prem Chand switched from Urdu to Hindi for similar reasons, and Yashpal chose Hindi rather than English, although Yashpal was more influenced than Prem Chand by the element of national pride.

Hindi literature grew with nationalism and made important contributions to its cause. The greatest Hindi author of his time was Prem Chand (1880–1936). He was profoundly influenced by Gandhian philosophy, and his earlier novels reflect his belief in the effectiveness of *satyāgraha,* the Gandhian idea that if the oppressed patiently endure suffering and love their oppressors, their love will melt the hearts of the oppressors. In Prem Chand's earlier novels, villains undergo a spiritual transformation. They give up their worldly goods and social position to build a just political and social order. However, in later years, Prem Chand (as well as Gandhi) was disillusioned, and his later novels have greater realism.

He always deplored violence, but never abandoned his attack on the weaknesses of Indian society—exploitation of the poor, untouchability, corruption of the priesthood. His writing reflected the two great movements of his time—the challenge to outmoded values in Indian society and the growth of national aspirations for freedom. His greatest gift was the compassion he felt for those he wrote about, especially the Indian peasant, who was poor and suffering, weak and superstitious, but had dreams of a better life. In his time, Prem Chand had no peer in Hindi literature.[5]

Yashpal, in his concern for the common man and commitment to social justice, his understanding of the quirks of human nature and ability to portray human beings with compassion and humor, and in his simple and powerful writing style, is heir to Prem Chand's place in Hindi literature.

Both men were deeply dedicated to their country's freedom; each responded to India's need according to his nature. Prem Chand channeled his energies into writing; Yashpal joined a revolutionary movement in the Punjab.

Gandhi opposed revolutionary tactics and under his leadership the Congress inherited the reins of power from the British. For this reason, the revolutionary movement has not often been appraised objectively. Therefore, it is worth quoting from the work of R. C. Majumdar, one of India's most eminent historians, who presents the view that the revolutionary movement has never received a fair share of credit for its role in achieving independence. He says:

> The cult of *Ahimsa* preached by Gandhi, and the current belief that it alone has brought independence to India, have stood in the way of a proper judgment

---

[5] A comprehensive analysis of Prem Chand's contribution to the short story in Hindi appears in *Premchand: A Critical Evaluation of Three Stages in the Evolution of one of the Foremost Hindi Short Story Writers,* by Robert Oscar Swan, Ph.D. dissertation, University of Pennsylvania, Philadelphia, 1966

of the nature of militant nationalism, which is generally styled violent methods in politics, and the role it played in the struggle for freedom . . .

Militant nationalism is generally referred to in official reports as terrorism. But, properly understood, it is merely the extreme branch of nationalism . . . But while nationalists relied upon passive resistance, like boycott, or other kinds of mass movement, one section of them regarded this also as inadequate for achieving the independence of India, and included violent action as a necessary part of the campaign against the British. These violent actions, carried out in secret, took various forms, according to inclination of the actors and their opportunities. One section adopted the programme of openly preaching revolution and murdering officials by pistols and bombs . . .

In Western countries perpetrators of political murders are not denounced, but regarded as heroes, and if they are caught and executed, they are looked upon as martyrs . . .

It will perhaps be news to many that eminent political leaders, both in England and India, did not fail to note the value of the terrorist cult in a freedom movement. When Madan Lal Dhingra shot dead Sir Curzon Wyllie in 1909, Lloyd George expressed highest admiration of his patriotism, and Churchill shared the view. So far as Indian leaders are concerned, we have now the evidence of the revolutionaries to the effect that their action was approved and encouraged by men like Aurobindo Ghosh, Surendranath Banerji, Aswini

Kumar Dutta, P. C. Ray, Lajpat Rai and Bal Gangadhar Tilak. Popular approval of these acts is still to be found in the folk songs about the martyrs in Bengal and other parts of India. In the face of all these it is hardly just to describe the so-called Terrorist Movement as the product of a few misguided youths. It was a great political movement, based upon European models, and sanctified by the blood, sacrifice and suffering of Indian youths, whose love for their motherland was proved by the supreme test—the one touchstone of real love—namely readiness to die for the object of love. Their martyrdom often touched the sublime . . .

As a matter of fact, the revolutionaries had two main objects in view. First, to awaken, by a rude shock, the inert mass of Indians from the political torpor of ages, and create a revolutionary mentality among the people; secondly, to paralyze, as far as possible, the effective work of administration, and to serve as a perpetual reminder of seething discontent of the Indians against the British rule. These objects were achieved to a large extent. Its indirect effect was also highly important. With the spread of revolutionary ideas large bands of young men—even those who did not actively participate in the revolutionary movement—were imbued with a new spirit of dedicating themselves to the service of the country at the cost of any suffering or sacrifice . . .

Further, it is also legitimate to hold, from such evidence as we possess, that the revolutionary activities had a great effect upon the British Government, and the Reforms of 1909 and the declaration of 1917 were largely influenced by them.[6]

A number of young freedom fighters in the Punjab joined a revolutionary movement because they regarded the Congress as an ineffectual body. In 1925, Bhagat Singh, who began his political activity as a Congress volunteer in the noncooperation movement, organized the Naujawan Bharat Sabha in Lahore for the purpose of political education and revolutionary activity.[7] In 1928, the revolutionaries of the Punjab, United Provinces, Rajputana and Bihar met in Delhi to consolidate the activities of the separate revolutionary organizations in Northern India. They formed the Hindustan Socialist Republican Army.[8]

The first act of the new organization was the boycott of the Simon Commission in Lahore. When the Commission reached Lahore, a huge procession led by Lala Lajpat Rai, the venerated "Lion of the Punjab," greeted it with a demonstration of black flags and cries of "Go back, Simon." The police attacked the procession with lathis and inflicted serious injuries on Lajpat Rai.[9] He died less than a month later, and his death is generally attributed to intense mental grief as well as

[6] R. C. Majumdar, *Three Phases of India's Struggle for Freedom*, Bombay: Bharatiya Vidya Bhavan, 1961, pp. 40–43

[7] Gopal Thakur, *Bhagat Singh, The Man and his Ideas*, New Delhi: People's Publishing House, 1962, p. 4

[8] This organization is sometimes referred to as the Hindustan Socialist Republican Association. In Hindi it is called the *Hindustān Samājvādī Prajātantra Senā*, and referred to by Yashpal in *Sinhāvalokan* by its initials, H.S.P.S. Here it will be referred to as the H.S.P.S.

[9] Gulab Singh, *Under the Shadow of Gallows*, Delhi: Roop Chand, 1963, p. 39

the physical injury he sustained.[10] The revolutionaries decided to avenge the murder of the great nationalist leader by killing the Deputy Superintendent of Police of the Punjab, Mr. Saunders.

> Chandra Shekhar Azad, Bhagat Singh, Kailashpati, Mahavir Singh, Kundanlal, Shivram, Rajguru, Yashpal and some others participated in the meeting which took this decision. On December 17, 1928, just a month after the death of the Sher-i-Punjab, Mr Saunders was killed in front of the police station near the D.A.V College, Lahore. Azad, Bhagat Singh, Rajguru and Jai Gopal carried out the action.[11]

The next activity of the H.S.P.S. was even more dramatic. Bhagat Singh and Batukeshwar Datta set off a bomb in the Legislative Assembly in Delhi to protest the Government's efforts to pass two repressive bills. Although the two men could have escaped, they chose to permit themselves to be arrested and to "make use of the court as a forum from which to proclaim their programme to the nation and rouse it to action." [12]

Shortly after the arrest of Bhagat Singh and Batukeshwar Datta, large bomb factories were discovered in Lahore and Saharanpur.[13] Mass arrests of the members of the H.S.P.S. followed, and the Lahore Conspiracy Case was instituted against them on July 10, 1929.

[10] Thakur, *op. cit.*, pp. 8–9
[11] Singh, *op. cit.*, p. 40
[12] Thakur, *op. cit.*, p. 12
[13] R. C. Majumdar, *History of the Freedom Movement in India,* Volume 3, Calcutta: Firma K. L. Mukhopadhyay, 1963, p. 517

Charges were framed against 32 persons but 7 of them turned approvers, and 9 including Chandra Shekhar Azad, Bhagwati Charan and Yashpal were declared absconders.[14]

In May 1930, a Special Tribunal was given summary powers to try the case. Bhagat Singh, Sukhdev, and Rajguru were sentenced to death in October 1930.

Although the H.S.P.S. was shattered by the large numbers of arrests and convictions in the Lahore Conspiracy Case, Yashpal and Azad, both of whom were fugitives, tried to carry on the work of the organization. In December 1929, the Viceroy was traveling to Delhi in his special train when an attempt was made on his life.

> . . . a bomb hidden beneath the track was detonated by Yashpal as the speeding train reached the explosive spot in the early hours of the morning. Only the dining car was blown to pieces, the Viceroy escaped unhurt.[15]

The police intensified their search for the two men. Azad was killed in Allahabad in February 1931. Yashpal tried to rally the few remaining revolutionaries, and was caught by the police and imprisoned in January 1932. His arrest effectively ended the revolutionary movement in the Punjab.[16]

Yashpal was sentenced to fourteen years at hard labor. This

[14] Singh, *op. cit.,* p. 41. "Approvers" are informers.

[15] Thakur, *op. cit.,* p. 36

[16] The focus of this paper is on Yashpal's writing, and the outline of events in his early life is intended to serve only as a frame of reference. Therefore, matters relating to H.S.P.S. activities are necessarily sketchy and incomplete.

was tantamount to a life sentence since, under the law, the prisoner was not automatically released at the end of his term, but could be kept in prison at the option of the government for his entire life.[17]

During the years of Yashpal's imprisonment, India moved toward self-government. In July 1937, Congress accepted ministries in seven provinces and declared that all political prisoners would be released without discrimination.[18] However, the revolutionaries were regarded by the British in a somewhat different category from the Congress Party prisoners, and initially assurance was sought from the revolutionaries that they had given up violence. Yashpal, as their spokesman, pointed out that a statement of this sort would imply that the object of the revolutionaries had, at one time, been violence. Furthermore, he indicated that if such a statement were made, a connection between the statement and the release of the prisoners would be established.[19] At this, no assurances were sought from the prisoners, and gradually they were released.

Yashpal was among the last to be freed. In March 1938, thanks to the devoted efforts of his wife, and owing in part to ill health, he was released from jail at the age of 35. He had given his youth to free his country. Now, with his own freedom regained and India's assured, he turned to a new career—writing.

[17] Yashpal, *op. cit.*, p. 137
[18] *Ibid.*, pages 182–83
[19] *Ibid.*, page 184

THE STORIES

TWO DESPERATE SOULS

An incident in Yashpal's life provided the background for "Two Desperate Souls" (Dukhī-Dukhī). The discovery by the police of the bomb factory in Lahore led to the prosecution of the Lahore Conspiracy Case in July 1929. Yashpal and Azad, declared absconders in the case, were hunted men. Nonetheless they tried to regroup the H.S.P.S. and carry on its work. In this connection, Yashpal traveled to Karachi to arrange with a former companion for the manufacture of an explosive. On his return to Delhi, he was almost caught by the police in the railway station at Hyderabad (Sind). He managed to escape and to make his way back to Delhi, but by the time he arrived there, he had not eaten for a long time and he had only six paisa in his pocket. Azad was out of the city, and Yashpal experienced the hunger and homelessness of the main character in "Two Desperate Souls."
He describes the events that inspired the story:

> So, hungry, I wandered about here and there . . . Well, when you have six paisa you can buy some parched gram or things like that . . . Although in those days I rarely smoked, I don't know what happened to me, but I went into a shop near Jama Masjid and bought a cigar for six paisa and, in the darkness of the evening, sat down in the maidan of the Parade Ground and began to smoke it . . . then I began to feel dizzy, probably from the cigar. I drank a lot of water from a tap near the mosque and on my empty

19

stomach, it made me feel worse. Then I lay down on the Parade Ground . . . In this long life of fifty years, I have seen a lot and done a lot, but this was the only time I have ever gone hungry for lack of money . . . I got up and started walking towards Ajmeri Gate through Chavari Bazaar and Fatehpuri. I passed by the Roshan Cinema House about 9:30 at night. In that part of town in those days, poor prostitutes lived in rooms on both sides of the street. The market was largely deserted by that hour so that when they saw me walking slowly, they thought I was a prospective customer. They started shouting from both sides of the street, "Hey, come here, come here!" I thought, "What if they are as hungry as I, and if I were to go to one of them, what would we say to each other?" This incident made so deep an impression on my mind, I could not forget it. Later on, in 1938 I wrote a story, Dukhī-Dukhī, on the basis of this experience, which was very well received by my readers.[20]

You squirm with embarrassment when you walk through red light districts like Tibbi Bazaar in Lahore, Dalmandi in Banaras, and Chavari in Delhi. Ah, now you wrinkle your nose in distaste. Why don't I feel that way? Listen . . .

You may not believe me, but I'm telling the truth . . . not a grain of food had passed my lips for four whole days. With each step I staggered, and waves of darkness rose and fell before my eyes. At first my head seemed to spin, then I

[20] Yashpal, *Sinhāvalokan*, Vol. 3, p. 25

thought it would explode with pain. Nausea overcame me; I had to vomit. But what was in my stomach? Only water. To put out the fire raging inside me, I went from one *pyau* [1] to another drinking water, but I could not keep any of it down. I would sit at the edge of the drains in the alleys, hold my head with both hands and retch. Passersby would stop and ask, "Say, what's the matter?" But the sight of me offended their delicate sensibilities, and they would cover their nose with a handkerchief, spit to one side, and hurry on.

I spent that first night in front of the railway station on a bench in the garden—what is it called—oh, yes—Victoria Gardens. I passed the second night on the bank of the Jamuna. By the third night my head ached miserably, my mind had begun to wander and my legs no longer had the strength to move. I don't know what I was seeking or of what blind hope I went by the Jama Masjid. Nearby, at the edge of the Parade Grounds, I saw some men preparing places to sleep on the footpath. There was no shortage of ground; nevertheless they were fighting over space, while through it all a *fakīr* [2] kept chanting and plucking away at an *iktārā*. [3]

Finding myself there, I felt as though I had come to the end of the road. Unlike the previous two nights, I no longer knew the shame which had driven me to seek a place to myself. I lay down alongside that litter of people. Oh, how a man can change so much, so quickly!

I began to wonder . . . what will happen now? . . . who will tell my family? But I had been thinking about that for three days and two nights already. I kept on thinking and

[1] A stand where water is provided for travellers.
[2] A Muslim holy man
[3] A one-stringed musical instrument

thinking until I was too exhausted to do anything but listen to
the conversation of some men lying nearby.

On the fourth day, I said to myself: What's the sense of
standing on false pride? Hundreds of people stretch out their
hands to beg; so shall I. Since Fate has snatched all I own, let
her have what is left of me.

But the moment I went near anyone, I couldn't utter a
word. I could only think—will this person even listen to my
story? From childhood, I had never asked anyone for anything, except my mother. She had told me: "Son, stand on
your own two feet. Never accept anything from anybody." I
realized now that she spoke with the pride of a full stomach.

Time after time I would go back to the railway station. It
was as though the station were the door to my home, but the
key to the door was money. The key I did not have—it was
lost. That is why I was a wanderer without a refuge.

From the station, I went to Fatehpuri. What crowds there
are in Fatehpuri in the evening! But of course you know that.
I kept floating along in the human current. I don't know what
drew me, what force kept dragging me back to the *purī-
parāthe*[4] stalls all evening long. I kept devouring the puris
with my eyes and longed to gulp them down in huge quanti-
ties. I was so famished that, passing by the kabob seller by the
side of the road, where formerly I had to hold my nose, now
the roasting meat made my mouth water. And I saw food
sticking to the leafplates that people were throwing away. My
hands almost reached for them, but I was wearing clothes,
and that realization stayed my hand. My self-respect had
vanished, but I still wore clothes.

[4] A kind of unleavened cake fried in ghee and made in several layers.

Hunger is an evil thing. It brings even elephants and lions to heel. How much can a human being endure? In an alley, I saw a devout Hindu woman feeding *roti*[5] to a bull.[6] I had to bite my lips to hold back my tears.

I continued to wander aimlessly, wherever my feet led, leaning on the walls for support. That is how I arrived at Hauz Kazi. Had I had my wits about me, I would have fled from that place without looking up. Instead, I meandered, looking around aimlessly. Why should I hesitate? I was devoid of sense and feeling.

The road from the Roshan Theatre to Ajmeri Gate is lined with shabby shops, and above them live poor prostitutes in murky little cells curtained by broken bamboo screens. That is where I roamed about.

Just as doctors, lawyers and shopkeepers are graded, so are prostitutes. One class lives in Chavari, where the upper-storied balconies are draped with garlands of flowers. Behind curtains of multi-colored sparkling glass beads, crystal chandeliers dazzle the eyes with their brilliance. The bazaar is fragrant with *khas*[7] and *hinā*.[8] From the rooms come the rippling music of the *tablā*,[9] *belā*[10] and *sārangī*,[11] playing to the jingling of anklet bells—and, breaking above the harmony, the clamor of laughter.

Another class of prostitute is down near the Roshan Theatre. There, lanterns strung from the eaves throw their feeble

---

[5] Bread
[6] The bull is a sacred animal and to feed it is a pious act.
[7] A kind of sweet-scented grass
[8] Henna
[9] small drums
[10] violin
[11] A four-stringed instrument resembling a guitar.

light on the dark walls and, like lizards who snatch the moths drawn by the light, the prostitutes with white-powdered faces sit and wait for their clients. Here and there a kerosene lamp disgorges smoke, and near it a hungry, desperate face with blank, staring eyes—waiting.

At times I had to drag my feet, and sometimes, to keep from falling, I would brace the small of my back with my hands and look around in all directions. Suddenly I felt as though someone were motioning to me from above. I looked up and saw several prostitutes calling to me from opposite sides of the street. This was the first time in four days anyone had beckoned to me.

I asked the one nearest to me on the right, "What do you want?" She answered quickly, "Whatever you wish to give."

"Give!" When I heard that word, my excitement died, but hers did not. She exclaimed, almost sobbing, "Oh, for God's sake, come up, come up!"

I know, after four days of endless hunger, a man loses all judgment and forgets who he is. I began to climb the stairs like a robot in answer to her call. My legs were shaky and I had to lean on the walls on either side for support. Even then I did not ask myself why I was going upstairs.

Though her hair was combed and braided, she looked no different from those people who were sleeping on the Parade Ground. A mat and a clay pitcher were the only furnishings of that wretched cubicle. At my questioning look, she broke out imploringly, "In the name of God, give me whatever you wish. I am dying. I have been here for four days, and I swear to God, in all that time I have not had a grain to eat."

I don't know why—I asked her, "How did you get here?"

Her misery spilled over. Weeping, she told me her husband

had beaten her and left her for another woman. She stayed in her house, crying and hungry for three days; then an "Auntie" [12] came and comforted her and brought her here. "Whatever I earn I split half and half. It is my Fate; not even one man came to me. I am dying of hunger. When Auntie came to light the kerosene lamp tonight, she patted me and said, 'Men will come.' "

I felt not the slightest scorn for her as she sat there offering her body for sale, I don't know why. I can't say whether my sense of right and wrong had died or whether the fire of my own hunger had purified her. Nor can I say today what I might have been willing to do on that day for just one *roti*.

Finding another human being in the same plight, I told her my sad tale—I, too, had not eaten for four days. My home is in Jullundur. After passing my exams, I was on my way to Calcutta to work in my uncle's business. I stopped for one day to see Delhi. My family had warned me against pickpockets in Delhi, so I put my money and ticket to Calcutta with all my belongings in a box and locked them in the little room of the inn, taking out just enough to buy food in the bazaar. When I returned after three hours of sightseeing, the room had been stripped clean. I panicked. I knew no one. I had no place to stay . . .

She turned to me with a beaten, despairing look and asked, "Then why did you come up here?" and burst out crying.

Getting down the stairs was even harder. I sat down on a step to catch my breath and thought, "What can one starving wretch give another? Only his misery."

[12] An employer of prostitutes

No sooner had I reached the street than a policeman stopped me and asked harshly, "What have you been up to?" I was silent—what could I say?

"What are you trying to get out of?" he persisted. Even then I could say nothing.

Then he said roughly, "You're coming to the police station. I'm arresting you under Section 109." [13]

What was "109" and what was "110," I didn't even know, but I had to go to the police station. Had I not been arrested, I probably would never have seen my home again.

The frightening image of the pot-bellied officer at the station shocked me into reality. Trembling all over, I said in English, "Sir, I am innocent."

That sentence spoken in English made everything all right. A telegram was sent home and everything was straightened out . . . but that last evening. . . .

That is why when I go by those places, I feel neither scorn nor shame.

[13] Section 109 of the Criminal Procedure Code deals with vagrancy.

THE BOOK OF EXPERIENCE

The lessons of life we learn in "The Book of Experience" per-
taining to the art of sharing and the art of composing differences
without recourse to government are reinforced in Gerald Berre-
man's ethnographic study of the Paharis, the Himalayan hill
people who are Yashpal's favorites and the subject of this story.
The Pahari culture area, defined as "the Himalayan foothills
from Kashmir across North India and Nepal," has many character-
istics which distinguish it from the Indo-Gangetic plain. The
differences encompass language, rituals, marriage rules, agri-
cultural practices, types of dwellings, and so forth. All Pahari
castes eat meat and drink liquor. Concerning marriage and the
behavior of women, the Pahari hill culture has:

> *A number of rules pertaining to marriage which would*
> *be unacceptable to many plains groups and especially to*
> *those of high caste. These include bride-price marriage*
> *with no necessity for a Sanskritic marriage ceremony,*
> *polyandry in some areas, levirate, divorce by mutual con-*
> *sent, remarriage of widows and divorcees, toleration of*
> *intercaste marriage within the high- or low-caste group.*
> *There is also a good deal of postmarital sexual freedom and*
> *sanctioned relations of brothers with one another's wives.*
> *. . . No seclusion of women and freer participation of*
> *women in most aspects of life than on the plains, includ-*
> *ing their participation in singing and dancing at festivals.*

Relatively free informal contact between the sexes is usual.[1]

With specific reference to the virtues of sharing in Sirkanda, the fictitious name for the hill village where he lived and studied in 1957 and 1958, Berreman notes:

> The most celebrated beauty of the Sirkanda area was a Brahmin girl of a neighboring village who was sexually available to Rajputs and Brahmins alike. What little critical gossip circulated about her was concerned with the frequency and openness of her contacts, not their inter-caste character . . . Her family raised no objection, and even her husband kept quiet. The analysis given by villagers was, "He can't say anything—if he did she might leave him and then he would have nothing. It is better to share something good than to lose it altogether.'[2]

The study gives further weight to the wisdom of the old woman concerning the activities of government officials. Of Pahari attitudes towards officialdom, it says:

> Contacts with outsiders have been limited largely to policemen and tax collectors—two of the most unpopular forms of life in the Pahari taxonomy. Such officials are despised and feared, not only because they make trouble for villagers in the line of duty, but also because they extort bribes on the threat of causing further trouble and often seem to take advantage of their official position to vent their aggressions on these vulnerable people. . . .[3]

[1] Gerald D. Berreman, *Hindus of the Himalayas*, Berkeley: University of California Press, 1963, Page 345
[2] *Ibid.* P. 230
[3] *Ibid.* P. 322

USUALLY it's helpful when people know who you are, but sometimes it's an advantage not to be known. I was traveling from Almora to Lohaghat.[1] There are only two ways to go there—on foot or on horseback. I was able to hire a gentle and attractive animal cheaply, so I rode. When traveling, I generally wear a khaki shirt and trousers so that my clothes won't look dirty and a hat for protection from the sun.

I was on the road about a mile beyond the shops of Ganchauki. It is a hard climb and the road winds and turns. Coming around a bend, I could see the cool shadow cast by a dense horse chestnut tree on the side of the road. Two elderly people, a woman and a man, were sitting on the ground in the shade a short distance from each other. It looked as though they had been walking together on the road and had stopped to rest and talk in the shade of the tree.

When the woman heard the clop-clop of the horse's hooves, shading her eyes from the sun with her hand, she looked at me and jumped up instantly as though she recognized me. She came toward the road, brushing off the dry leaves and grass which had stuck to her skirt from sitting on the ground.

[1] The journey from Almora to Lohaghat is fifty-three miles through the hill country of Uttar Pradesh in the foothills of the Himalayas. It is an area famous for the refreshing qualities of its climate and people.

The man followed a few steps behind her. When I saw them coming toward me, I reined in the horse.

"Are you the Joint Sahib,[2] Maharaj?"[3] the old woman raised her hands in greeting.

I shook my head and asked her in the dialect of the Almora hills, "Why? Is the Joint Sahib coming?"

She sighed as though a great weight had been lifted from her head. Relieved of the burden of gathering her courage to address the Joint Sahib, she relaxed. She put her hands on her hips, looked reassuringly at her companion and said to me, "Then who are you? You must be some kind of big man!"

Before I could answer, her companion volunteered his opinion. "He must be a big lawyer from the city."

"Well then," the old woman put her finger on her chin and turning to her companion, said, "It is just such big people as this who can help us in our difficulties . . . what do you say, brother . . . isn't that so?"

"Of course, of course," her companion attested to her wisdom.

"Why, what happened?" I asked sympathetically.

"Nothing happened, Maharaj," with a deep sigh the old woman extended her arms out to their full length in a gesture to demonstrate that she was not concealing anything. "What happened? Nothing happened, but nonetheless there is something. . . . Well, that is always the way. . . . It happens all the time . . . People make a mountain out of a molehill . . . And now what can be done? . . . . Even though it was really nothing . . . It's madness, that's all it is."

[2] Term designates a high government official. Here it refers to the Magistrate.
[3] Term of respect

"Why, what is the trouble?" Her embarrassment and the combination of her eagerness and reluctance to talk about it so sharpened my curiosity that I repeated the question.

"Ah, Maharaj, trouble?" the woman answered in a deeply thoughtful way, "there was no trouble, but trouble was made of it. It was nothing very serious, but something serious has come of it. That wife of Moti Dholiya—well, Bahadur Dholiya has taken her to live with him. That was all. But it was reported to the police. Doesn't that shame the whole village? And besides the disgrace, what will happen? Everyone will be dragged into the quarrel."

The old woman threw up her hands as she explained, "That was the whole thing, but is that how things should be done? Maharaj, it happens everywhere! Where does it not happen? From the king's palace to the humblest peasant's hut, it happens. But, Maharaj, there is a way to handle everything. Everyone does. . . . Who hasn't done it? . . . . Didn't I do it in my time? . . . Haven't you done it? . . . But there is a proper way to do things."

The old woman looked into my eyes confidingly, and went on, "Maharaj, what is a man? He is just like a bee. Round and round he flies. It is the woman, sitting open and blooming like a flower, who calls to him. Maharaj, when the bee sees the open, blooming flower, he comes. How can he help it? Then it is up to the woman to do what is to be done and how it should be done. Maharaj, a woman as old as I am . . . what have I not done? What have I not seen? But if a woman has a way, everything can be done, and no one will have an inkling of it.

"See how crude those people are! They will bring misfortune on the entire village. A man is not an animal that he has to frighten others by showing his horns and growling. A man must accommodate another man, don't you think so, Maharaj? Now the clumsiness and stupidity of one person will result in misery for all. The madness of that Moti Dholiya! . . . If it is not madness, what is it? . . . Ah, well, he is still very young.

"If you find the water in the lake sweet, well sir, scoop up handfuls of it and drink it properly. But do you really think you can put the whole lake in your pocket and take it away with you? That would be unbecoming both to the lake and you."

The old woman held both hands to her head and said helplessly, "What can I say, Maharaj? I don't want to say anything, but I can't help saying it. It's a matter which concerns the whole village." She sighed deeply and went on, "It is all madness—nothing but madness. Anyone who does such a crazy thing should be considered a lunatic and shunned. If not today, then tomorrow he'll fall on his face and realize his mistake. But now that a report has been made, the Joint Sahib will come and turn the village into chaos. After all, that is his job. He's an official, isn't he? Officials look for such opportunities. For such things they come all the way from the city. Maharaj, a government servant is like a fly. He searches everywhere for a pile of filth so that he can sit down on it. If the fly doesn't find filth, the poor thing will die. That is the way of a government official, but that is not the way of a gentleman. A gentleman is one who, when he sees another person exposed, covers him with his own cloth. But government officials search for holes in the cloth to poke their fingers through. And what do you think of someone who goes to them and points out the holes himself. . . . ?"

At first, as I listened to the woman's story, I felt so tickled I wanted desperately to laugh. But in my eagerness to learn more, I suppressed my laughter by biting my lips and looking very serious. By the time she finished, I felt shame and disgust at my earlier reaction. The standard of decent behavior which she presented made me shrink at the thought of laughing at another person's embarrassment or difficulties.

I expressed my sympathy to her and spurred the horse on. I began thinking about the incident. Social scientists have written that "government is a necessary evil." What socialist or anarchist knows this truth better than that woman? Socialists and anarchists have read only printed books, but this woman has read the book of experience . . .

A NAME FOR THE PAINTING

*Men who dedicate themselves to causes are not usually noted
for gentle humor and tongue-in-cheek wit. Yashpal is an excep-
tion. He is intrigued by the pretensions of artistic temperament,
and with humor and perception describes a personality we all
recognize. In "A Name for the Painting" (Citr kā Shīrṣak), it is
Jayraj, the artist who feels it is his right to enjoy Beauty since he
requires it in order to create. No matter if the Beauty is his good
friend's wife! For as Jayraj says, "Without the nectar of the flower,
how can the bee make honey?"*

*Yashpal loves the hills of Northern India and makes them the
setting for many of his stories. The events on which this story
turns take place in Ranikhet in the Almora District of Uttar
Pradesh. Ranikhet has been a military cantonment for nearly a
century, but in recent years its charms as a hill resort have been
discovered.*

*For Jayraj, the visit to Ranikhet was for reasons of artistic in-
spiration, for Nita a haven from the heat of the plains, but for
those who make their living from the land, the peasants of the
hills whom Jayraj painted, it is a hard life. Spate says:*

> *The basis of life in Kumaon is elaborately organized agri-
> culture . . . The terracing is often most elaborate, cover-
> ing entire hillsides with steps 5–8 feet high (occasionally
> up to 20 feet) and 10–20 feet wide . . . Since it takes a day
> for one man (assisted by others to fetch the stone) to build
> a wall a foot thick, six long and three high, the cumulative*

*labour involved is enormous. Maintenance also is arduous in a region where even properly built roads are often swept away by landslips.**

J AYRAJ was a famous and successful artist. To capture nature and life in Ranikhet with the fidelity his art demanded, he moved there at the very beginning of April. At that time of year the mountain air is crystal clear and the sky is always blue. Viewed from Ranikhet, the snowy peaks of *Trishūl, Pancacūli* and *Caukhambā* [1] pierce the brilliant sky. They sparkle as though the deep blue sea had surged and swelled to splash the roof of the sky, sprinkling pearls and gems studded in the white foam scooped from its depths onto the mountains beneath.

Jayraj painted a number of these scenes, but they left him empty. They lacked the spark of humanity, and he felt like one who plays a raga [2] in a wasteland. Where were the struggles and aspirations of mankind?

Then he saw some peasants working in their fields, which were ribbed along the slope of the mountain, and he painted them. But still he was not fulfilled. A cry of anguish born of the failure of his art rose within him He had to paint the

---

* O.H.K. Spate, *India & Pakistan: A General and Regional Geography,* London: Methuen & Co. Ltd., 1963, page 404–5

[1] Poetic imagery. *Trishūl* is a trident or three-pronged lance. *Caukhambā* means four pillars. *Pancacūli* stands for five hinges.

[2] song; musical composition

dreams and longing of his heart, but he could not. Driven by
the need to express himself, he sat restlessly on the veranda,
chin in hand, facing the undulating valley bathed in the
golden sunlight that filtered through the trees, looking aimlessly at the silver strands of rivers winding through the deep
ravines to the milk-foam on the mountain. He had no particular objective; his eyes simply wandered over the broad sweep.
Suddenly a young woman, graceful and elegant, appeared on
the slope of the mountain. She was here, there and everywhere—wherever he looked in that vast expanse.

Jayraj felt oddly reassured. He sighed deeply and shut his
eyes tight, hoping to prolong the sight. He was like a man
drifting along on an endless sea, bereft of all hope of rescue,
who suddenly hears a voice calling to him. He said to himself,
"This is what I need. If I am to create Beauty, I, myself, must
experience the joy of Beauty." Without the nectar of the
flower, how can the bee make honey?

As he pondered this problem, a letter arrived. It was from
his friend Somnath, a lawyer in Allahabad. The two had
become acquainted through Somnath's admiration and respect for Jayraj's art. In fact, they had become close friends.
Somnath begged the pardon of the famous artist for this
intrusion on his precious time, and then went on to say of his
wife, "Nita is in very poor health this year, and I want her to
stay in the mountains for a few months. The weather is
unbearably hot here in Allahabad and she is very uncomforta-
ble. If you could arrange for a nice, small house nearby that
would be inexpensive, I will send her there. If you have
possibly rented an entire house to yourself and have space to
spare, and if it would not interfere with your work, we could
sublet two or three rooms. We would send another servant to
look after Nita . . . etc. etc."

When Jayraj had been in Allahabad two years ago, Som gave a tea party in his honor. Som and Nita had been married only a few months then. In the crush of the crowd at the party, Jayraj was barely able to exchange a few words with her. He ransacked his memory. He could recall only a slender, supple body, a fair complexion, gay manner and eyes that sparkled with intelligence. Jayraj set the letter aside and thought, "What shall I say?"

He looked out over the valley, but in his mind's eye he saw Nita sitting in an armchair sharing the view with him, and now and then looking down at the book in her hand. That make-believe young woman seated next to him stirred in him more powerful emotions than the beauty of all the snow-clad, radiant, crystal-brilliant mountain peaks stretched out before him. The tantalizing fragrance of her hair and body captivated him far more than the perfume of the *sevati* [3] and *sirish* [4] flowers borne on the breeze from the valley.

In his imagination he saw Nita climbing up a path in the valley ahead of him. The way is strewn with sharp stones and pebbles, and she holds up her sari, showing her rosy, sandaled heels and her calves, delicate and golden as the stalk of the plantain tree. She is beginning to breathe heavily, and with each breath her breasts swell and strain against her choli reminding him of the sudden tearing of the lotus sheath when the flower bursts into bloom. [5]

[3] white rose; eglantine.

[4] A deciduous, fast-growing tree with fragrant flowers.

[5] The comparison of swelling breasts to lotus buds is common in Sanskrit literature. Ashvaghosa refers to Nanda's mistress in "Sundara Nanda" by comparing her to a lotus pond, "with her laughter for the swans, her eyes for the bees, and her swelling breasts for the uprising lotus buds . . ." See M. S. Randhawa, *Flowering Trees in India,* New Delhi: Indian Council of Agricultural Research, 1957, Page 12.

Now he sees himself before his easel. Nita wants to pass through the room, and to avoid disturbing him, she tiptoes quietly behind him. He hears her speaking to the servant and the sound of her voice fills the void in his heart with ecstasy.

Jayraj picked up his pen and began to reply. Then he stopped and asked himself, "What do I want? What do I want of my friend's wife?" He considered all the possibilities objectively and concluded, "Why, nothing at all!" Just as we do not pounce upon the sunbeams in the sunshine, for their mere radiance fulfills our needs, so in his time of dark loneliness, Jayraj felt that the brightness of a woman's presence was all he wanted.

He sent a short note. "I have rented an entire house away from the crowds. It has a great deal of extra room. Subletting is out of the question. An old family servant is here with me and if Nita can keep an eye on things, her visit will be a favor to me. Bring her as soon as you can. Let me know when you are arriving so that I can meet you at the bus depot."

The anticipation of that beautiful girl so close to him made Jayraj's heart dance. His memory of her was vague at first, but by applying his artistic ideals of beauty, Jayraj sharpened her image. He began to see her with him on the veranda, in the valley, on the mountain path. His fantasy dressed her in saris of different colors, in *salvār* and *kamīz*,[6] in a skirt and blouse. He framed her in a bower of blossoming vines, in the shade of the deodars, under a pine tree. He found her everywhere. And he became impatient waiting for her to appear in reality as a man plunged in darkness longs for the sunlight.

[6] *Salvār* and *kamīz* are typical Punjabi dress for women. The *salvār* are trousers which are generally full in the leg and the *kamīz* is a long overblouse.

Som's reply came by return mail indicating the date of Nita's arrival and saying, "I have to appear in High Court that day. The heat is fierce here and it is getting worse. I don't want Nita to suffer any longer. She has a reserved seat on the train to Kath Godam, and I have told her to take a taxi from there to avoid the crowded buses. Will you please meet her at the station? You have done so much for us already, may I ask for this one small added favor? We are both so grateful. . . ."

Jayraj arrived at the bus station early, eager to spare his friend's cultivated and sensitive wife any distress. His eyes were glued to the turn in the road where the taxis from Kath Godam suddenly emerge from behind the hill. There it was! Jayraj ran toward the taxi. It stopped.

There in the back he saw a lady spread out over the seat, her body unable to support its weight. Exhaustion and illness had yellowed her complexion and dark circles underlined her dull eyes. Jayraj looked—stared! At the flicker of recognition in her glance and her offering of *namaskār*,[7] he was forced to acknowledge, "I am Jayraj." The lady made an effort to smile. "I am Nita." It was the smile of *noblesse oblige*—a lady does what is proper no matter how awful the cost.

The burden she bore in front made it extremely difficult for her to maneuver herself out of the car onto her thin legs. She could hardly manage her body which seemed to be flopping all about, just as on a journey it is difficult to control a bedroll when the strap has broken. She had barely hobbled a few steps when Jayraj summoned a *ḍāṇḍī*,[8] which, with Nita, was placed on the shoulders of four men. Courtesy dictated that

[7] A greeting indicated by joining the palms of the hands.
[8] A chair conveyance used in the hills, generally for transporting sick people.

he walk alongside the *ḍāṇḍī,* but just to be near that gross, disgusting shape nauseated and depressed him.

The moment they arrived at the house, Nita went to her room to lie down. The constant moaning coming from that room shattered Jayraj's nerves. He stuck his fingers in his ears to get some relief, but her groans seemed to penetrate every pore of his body. If only he could blot out of his consciousness Nita's ugly form—the bloated, bulging mass sagging under its own weight. But that image could not be banished from his sight. His entire house was permeated with her presence. He had to get away, anywhere—far, far away.

Next morning, when the sun's first rays glinted on the veranda and there was still a cold nip in the air, Jayraj sat down to relax in an easy chair far from Nita's room. Bored with her prolonged bedrest, Nita, too, dragged herself out into the fresh air. She lowered herself into the other armchair, and as she suppressed a sigh, inquired about Jayraj's health, and then went on to say, "Perhaps it was the journey that wore me out or perhaps the strange bed—I don't know which—but I didn't sleep a wink last night." Jayraj could not sit there another moment. He stood up, saying he would return shortly, and fled. He wandered about for miles, up one path and down another in sheer frustration, seeking deliverance from this calamity. He felt like a trapped bird frantically flapping its wings in the birdcatcher's net.

He saw a way out.

Rushing to the postoffice, he sent Som a telegram: "Have received wire from Banaras that Mother is sick and asking for me. Must leave immediately. Rent paid for six months. Servant will stay here. If you can, come and stay with your wife."

Returning to the house, he had the servant pack a few things for him saying he would be gone for a couple of days, and instructed him to show Nita the telegram to Som after his departure. His parting words were, "Madam is not to be inconvenienced in any way."

Som wrote to Jayraj from Ranikhet, deeply concerned about his friend's mother. The High Court was now in recess and he and Nita were eagerly awaiting Jayraj's return. Jayraj replied, thanking him, urging him to stay on in Ranikhet and to regard the house and servant as his own. As for himself, several matters prevented him from returning soon. Som wrote again and again, but Jayraj did not come back to Ranikhet. Finally, Som and Nita went home to Allahabad, and Jayraj ordered his servant to return to Banaras with his belongings.

Now Jayraj no longer suffered from loneliness; he was sick with revulsion at the realization that Beauty is a fraud. He was obsessed with life's ugliness. He could not free his mind of the sight and sound of Nita—her illness, her bloated belly, her whining. He went straight to Kashmir, determined to rid himself of the horror which filled his soul. Once again he floated on a houseboat ringed by lotus flowers in the blue Dal Lake, and as he gazed at the snow-topped mountains, yearned that the passion for beauty be restored to him. Then he went to the seacoast to watch the ebb and flow of the tide in the silver moonlight. He tried to lose himself in the cities, pounding with the struggle for survival—but the hideous reality which filled his mind haunted him.

Back to Banaras. With brush and paint on canvas he sought vengeance for the outrage inflicted on him. Jayraj

painted a picture of Nita, swollen and twisted, lying across a
bed. The eyes in her sallow face bulged with pain and a cry
escaped her bitten lips.

Just as he was giving the picture its final touches, a letter
arrived from Som, insisting Jayraj come to Allahabad to cele-
brate his son's Naming-Day[9] ceremony. Jayraj cursed, crum-
pled the invitation and threw it on the floor. Then, for propriety, he answered with a postcard saying, "Best wishes and
congratulations! I want so much to come, but right now, I,
myself, am not too well. All my blessings to the baby!"

The postcard from their esteemed and warm-hearted friend
reached Som and Nita on Saturday. They took the next train
to Banaras and arrived at Jayraj's house early Sunday morning. The servant took them into his studio. Directly in front
of them as they entered the room stood the finished picture.
They looked at it and looked at it and could not look away
from it. Jayraj wished he could sink into the earth. The
enormity of his offense so shamed him that he did not dare to
face his guests. When he finally looked at Nita, he saw her
covering her lips with the edge of her sari to hide her laughter
as she held the gurgling baby to her breast. Her eyes sparkled
with triumph and amusement, while shyness and joy were
blended in the blush of her cheeks. How much more enchant-
ing was this Nita who stood before him than the Nita of his
fantasy in Ranikhet! Jayraj was shattered. Deceived again!
Once more his heart was filled with rage at this betrayal! Just

---

[9] One of the Hindu sacraments. On the twelfth day after the birth of a
child, it is given a name. This is called the *nāma-karma* ceremony. The
father of the child invites relatives and friends to be present at the
ceremonies and at the feast which follows them.

as he raised his knife to destroy the painting, he heard Nita purr, "What have you named the picture?"

Jayraj's hand stopped in midair. Seeing her expression of satisfaction, he was struck dumb and motionless.

Since it was apparent that the artist could not think of a suitable title for the superb painting, she proudly held up the baby to him and suggested, smiling, "Why not call it *The Agony of Creation?*"

SÂG [1]

Sāg is the most revealing story of this collection. In a few pages we learn a great deal about Yashpal's attitudes toward the British rulers, his own countrymen and the revolutionaries.

The setting is the August 1942 uprising in India. Two Indians have been sentenced to hang for killing an Englishman and his family.

British punctiliousness is brought out: The prisoners' wounds are dressed. They are held for trial. The trial is held, though its outcome is assured. Even an appeal to the High Court is made in their behalf.

Toward his countrymen, Yashpal is ambivalent. He points out that a handful of British rule hundreds of millions of Indians only because the Indians themselves aid in the rule. The police, the jailers, the soldiers are Indian. The British look with loathing at the prisoners; the Indian jailers do not look at them at all. The men who are about to die wonder for whom they are making their sacrifice. They go to the gallows without the comfort of a friendly glance from their own countrymen. However, Yashpal points out that their sacrifice has indeed awakened a spark in those for whom they died.

[1] Sāg literally means greens in the sense of green, leafy vegetables. There did not seem to be a satisfactory translation which would retain the original impact in Hindi. Therefore I kept the Hindi title.

Although Sāg *is set at the time of the August 1942 uprising, the events depicted in the story are reminiscent of the trial and execution of Bhagat Singh, Rajguru and Sukhdev in 1931—their summary trial, the rumors which followed their execution to the effect that their bodies had been desecrated, and the refusal of the authorities to give the bodies of the revolutionaries to their families for fear of providing an opportunity for public demonstration.*

At that time, Bhagat Singh was a popular hero. In fact, Sitaramayya in the official history of the Congress Party says:

> It is no exaggeration to say that at that moment Bhagat Singh's name was as widely known all over India and as popular as Gandhi's.[2]

Public agitation at the death sentence was so great that Gandhi was persuaded to seek commutation from the Viceroy, Lord Irwin.[3] The date of the execution had been fixed for March 24, 1931.[4] However, the British government feared that the public might demonstrate in front of the jail on that day, demand the bodies and carry them in a procession by way of protest against the government.

> Therefore, to forestall all these possibilities, with the permission of the Governor, they decided it would be better to have the matter done and over with before all that.[5]

Yashpal says that as a result of this decision, the prisoners were taken out of their cells to be hanged on March 23. First they were to be handcuffed. Sukhdev protested this, but an old Indian jailer appealed to Bhagat Singh, saying, "Please be kind to us. We have been ordered to handcuff you, and that is a rule of the jail. Please

[2] B. Pattabhi Sitaramayya, *The History of the Indian National Congress,* Volume 1, (1885–1935), Bombay: Padma Publications Ltd. 1946, Page 456

[3] R. C. Majumdar, *History of the Freedom Movement in India,* Volume 2, Calcutta: Firma K. L. Mukhopadhyay, 1963, page 383

[4] Yashpal, *op. cit.,* page 81

[5] *Ibid.*

comply with it." Bhagat Singh urged Sukhdev and Rajguru to agree to be handcuffed and when they all were, Bhagat Singh said to his comrades, "Well, brothers, let's go." As they walked into the prison yard, from every cell there came the shout over and over again, "Inkalāb zindābād!" [6]

Their last request was that they might have two minutes in which to say what they wished. The Superintendent, by his silence, assented. All three shouted, "Long live revolution! Down with imperialism!" [7] *Then they mounted the scaffold and were hanged.*

> *That day no food was eaten in the entire jail. Perhaps the Indian officers of the jail who served the Government could not eat that day out of remorse or conscience—or perhaps even out of grief.* [8]

A few days after the execution, the Indian National Congress met in Karachi and a rumor was current among the Congress members to the effect that:

> *. . . the remains of the late Sirdar Bhagat Singh and Sriyuts Raj Guru and Sukhadev were otherwise dealt with in an insulting manner. Accordingly the Working Committee appointed a Committee to examine the allegations forthwith and to report to the Working Committee on or before the 30th April. We may at once state that Bhagat Singh's father, who was largely responsible for the step taken was not able to produce any evidence in that behalf nor did he appear before the Committee to help it in any manner. Accordingly nothing resulted.* [9]

Concerning public reaction to the execution, Yashpal says:

> *The hearts of the people were filled with intense and helpless hatred toward the foreign government. As a result, people spread stories about the cruelties which were in-*

[6] Long live revolution!
[7] Yashpal, *op. cit.* page 83
[8] *Ibid.*
[9] Sitaramayya, *op. cit.* page 465

flicted on Bhagat Singh and his companions and of the courage with which they faced the gallows. To show their hatred and anger towards the government and their reverence for the martyrs, people would exaggerate these stories, and those who heard them would add something more, and that is how these stories gained currency.[10]

Concerning the disposition of the bodies of the revolutionaries, Yashpal says:

There was no hope that the government would give the bodies of the martyrs to their relatives so that they might honor them. However, the people intended to make sure that the government did not take the bodies far away and treat them disrespectfully or neglect them. So people sat on every road which left Lahore. Bhagat Singh's sister, Amarkaur, was on the Phirozpur Road with some friends. They saw police lorries going towards Phirozpur at about midnight and realized that the bodies of the heroes were being taken to the Satlaj River about sixty-five miles from Lahore. Before daybreak, many people were already on the railway bridge on the Satlaj. Three funeral pyres were still burning, but the police had returned. A large crowd gathered there during the day. Reverently, people took whatever they could from there—a little ash from the funeral pyres or some burnt bones. Every year in March until 1947, a fair was held there. It is part of Pakistan now.

There were some rumors that the police had desecrated the bodies, that is to say that, before cremating them, they had hacked them to pieces, and that Hindu rites had not been performed. To remove that impression from the public mind, the government issued a notice that very evening saying that the last rites of Bhagat Singh, Sukhdev and Rajguru had been performed by a Sikh priest and a Brahmin priest, and that their funeral pyres had been built in proper places on the bank of the river. People did not have much faith in what the government said, but those

[10] Yashpal, *op. cit.*, page 81

who knew the ways of the British government did not believe that they would mutilate a body. For what would be the point of doing that? The English rulers were always concerned that they not be regarded as barbarians and not give the people any reason to become aroused unnecessarily, and that there be a kind of show of justice and legal morality and procedure and all that. They felt that such behavior was necessary in order to maintain control over the Indian police and army.[11]

THEY locked up Visheshar Prasad and Rahman Khan in the death cells of the District Jail. The English Collector, who was in the District to restore law and order after the uprising, and the honorable English Civil Surgeon stood in front of the bars and stared at the prisoners. These two were not like circusgoers looking at the lions and cheetahs in their iron cages. They stared, neither with wonder nor with curiosity, but with stark hatred.

Both prisoners had been shot before they were captured. The English Civil Surgeon, as his duty dictated, removed the bullets from Visheshar Prasad's knee and Rahman Khan's stomach and dressed their wounds. As he performed his duty, the sahib's face shriveled up with hate like a withered date. His Indian staff, tense and deferential, danced attendance on him—the jailer, the jail doctor, the druggist, the jail clerks

[11] *Ibid.* pages 83–84

and guards—while he repeated over and over in his "tooti footi"[1] Hindustani, "These filthy swine set fire to the houses of the sahibs and murdered them in cold blood."

The Collector ordered the prisoners' legs shackled even before their bullet wounds had healed. Then they were charged, and the Sessions Judge, himself, came and held the trial in the jail. Evidence was produced immediately, proof was established, and they were sentenced to hang for the crimes of murder and arson.

According to the law of the Government, an appeal is made to the High Court on behalf of every person sentenced to death. An appeal was made even for these men. The High Court could set aside the death sentence or stamp it with its seal of approval. In the meantime, the prisoners waited behind iron bars.

Whenever the English Civil Surgeon had to pass their cells, his face contorted with loathing. All he could do was snarl, "Murderers!" and spit. Taking their cue from the sahib, the Indian jailer and all the other officials and guards treated these vicious criminals even more harshly. No other prisoner was allowed to step within the shadow of their cells. When the guards themselves walked past the cells, they went by with faces blank and hard as stone.

Visheshar Prasad and Rahman Khan realized the gravity of their crime. They had no hope of pardon. But in despair they wondered—why did all these Indians hate and fear them? They had been fighting the Government of the English, but the Englishmen of that Government were few and rarely seen. That Government was run by Indians like these. If the country is to be freed, then from whom?

[1] Broken; fractured.

The anger of the sahibs, their hatred for the murderers and their passion for vengeance was limitless. The moment the High Court approved the death sentence, all the English officials in the District came at dawn to watch the condemned men twitch on the hanging rope.

The prisoners faced Death. The avenging enemy flung them to Him. To keep the spirit of freedom alive in the face of the vengeance which was claiming their bodies, and so to cheat defeat, they shouted as they climbed the gallows, "Long live the Revolution! Victory to Mother India!" They looked all around them at the Indians who stood immobile and expressionless as wooden images. Even at the last instant of life, they were not offered one sign of kinship from their own people, and died seeing only the bitterness on the faces of the enemy.

The weeping relatives of Visheshar and Rahman waited at the jail gate to claim the bodies of their men, but the Collector refused to give them up. He feared a public display of the corpses might shatter the public peace. The Civil Surgeon ordered the Indian jailer, "The rebels are to be buried inside the jail compound," and, through clenched teeth, added, "Plant *marsā*² on the corpses. When it comes up send it to all the sahibs."

Marsā grows very quickly. Pushing up through the deep, well-turned earth, it grew even more quickly. The Civil Surgeon watched its progress day after day, and when he saw the

---

² *Marsā* is a specific kind of *sāg*. Botanically, it is amaranthus oleraceus. It does not appear to have an English name.

sāg was just right, he ordered it sent to the other sahibs. The news flew through the jail. The *sāg* on the graves has been sent to the sahibs today.

The jail was locked at night. The *sāg* preyed on the mind of every prisoner shut up in his cell. Each one imagined: The English are eating the Indians. But no one said a word. What if someone were to report such talk to the sahibs?

Every officer in the jail was thinking about the *sāg*. In the mind of each one was this thought: The English are eating the Indians. The jailer in his milky-white mosquito netting under the punkah, his heart seething, buried his face in the pillow. The doctor and the druggist, their heads under the sheet, lay awake in the dark. From the Head Guard, lying on a torn and filthy blanket, his eyes shut tight, to the newest 20-rupee-a-month recruit, face down on his battered charpoy, a single thought was in the minds of all, but not a word passed anyone's lips.

That evening, the sahibs celebrated the restoration of order in the District with a dinner at the Club. On crystal platters, Indian bearers served the *sāg* nourished by the bodies of the Indian rebels. They, too, knew the story of the *sāg*. Their faces were drawn with terror and their legs were weak and trembling, but their hands, out of fear, kept working like machines in the service of the sahibs.

The thought that tormented every heart remained unspoken—out of fear of the sahibs—out of fear of one another. A cry of anguish rose in every heart, but each single cry was scattered like a dead sigh dissolving in the wind. Even if all the separate cries united, they would have less than half the power such cries could muster had the people not feared one another. FEAR! Fear of themselves, fear of the enemy, fear everywhere. . . .

THE ESSENCE OF LOVE

"The Essence of Love" (Prem kā Sār) *demonstrates Yashpal's effective handling of all types of people. Here the life of an illiterate peasant woman of Kashmir is told in her own words and, by way of contrast, her life is viewed through the eyes of a sophisticated big-city police inspector.*

He is looking for dope smugglers and she appears to him a prime suspect. After all, she has come to Lahore all alone and understands no word of Punjabi. She clutches a small bundle to her breast. Does the bundle contain dope? No—just a man's embroidered vest, the kind that bridegrooms wear. What is her story?

She has come to Lahore to find her husband, who left her thirty years ago. Over the years he has written to her only for money, and she has mortgaged the land, sold the stock, and spent her life alone, but her memories of him remain fresh and warm. The Police Inspector finds her husband and brings him to her. What happens when a thirty-year illusion is shattered by reality?

THOSE were the days when the charas-smuggling [1] from
Peshawar had grown to such frightful proportions that
the customs police were being driven to desperation. There
was no letup day or night. It took far more ingenuity to catch
a dope smuggler than other types of criminals. For one thing,
it was impossible to anticipate the form the charas would be
in and where it would be hidden.

As I walked up and down the main station in Lahore, I
kept a sharp eye on the passengers getting off the Peshawar
Express. An old woman, looking confused, walked toward me
right in the middle of the road. She was wrapped from head
to toe in a long shawl. One look at that woman aroused my
suspicions. Having worked for so long on the police force, I
have learned this much: Where there is nothing to suspect,
then you should be doubly suspicious. How many times in

[1] "Bhang, charas and ganja are manufactured from the hemp plant
which is indigenous to the country. Its cultivation is not prohibited, but it
is understood that only the fibre and the seeds are to be used, the production of drugs being now illegal. This latter prohibition does not, however,
carry much force, for it is impossible to prevent the extraction of charas.
Charas is the resinous exudation from the ripe leaves, stems and seeds of
the female plant, and it can be made by the simple process of rubbing these
parts of the plant in the hand." H. G. Walton, Editor, *District Gazetteer
of the United Provinces,* Vol. XXXV, Government Press. U.P. Allahabad,
1928, page 154.

the luggage of *burka-*[2]clad ladies of the best families have seers[3] of charas been discovered! What if some rascal was using this woman to smuggle several seers of charas? That would be nothing new!

"Hey, mother. Say, old woman! Come here," I called to her. She pressed a little bundle to her bosom with one hand and tightened the shawl about her with the other. She glanced in my direction but pretended she hadn't heard me and kept going on her way.

Now I had real reason for suspicion. I called sharply, "Come here!" She appeared neither to hear nor to understand. Taking a quick look in my direction, she continued on. The constable who was with me stepped in front of her and stopped her.

I pointed to the little bundle in her hand and asked, "What is in it?" She gestured vaguely and babbled something in an anxious tone. I could make nothing of it at all. Sensing some trickery, I repeated my question in Pashto. Agitated, she said something pleadingly, but I couldn't understand a word of it.

I was at a loss. Was this woman pretending to be mad? Was it possible that she really did not understand Punjabi or Pashto, but actually spoke another language? Trying to make her understand, the constable with me snapped in a loud voice, "What is in it?" But he got nowhere.

Then I thought, if this woman is so ignorant, how could she have traveled to a place like Lahore alone on the Peshawar Express, and at night, too? And why? What business does she have here? I was completely nonplussed. Just then,

---

[2] A loose, enveloping garment, usually with veiled eyeholes, worn in public by Muslim women.

[3] A unit of weight equal to 2.057 pounds.

Kasim, my policeman-companion, gesturing in that direction with both hands, asked in Kashmiri, "Are you from Kashmir?" With a long sigh she said yes.

Now we knew she was a Kashmiri, but there could still be charas in her bundle, or was there perhaps some other mystery about her? What proof is there that she is not one of that gang of Kashmiri smugglers who slip in and out of Lahore? Just the way she couldn't take her hand off that bundle left me no alternative but to suspect her. Kasim asked her, "Where were you going?" But still no answer.

Kasim said, "Sir, this wretch is up to something." I thought for awhile, then told him to put her in a tonga and take her to the main police station. She protested loudly, but she finally got into the tonga.

Pir Husain was a constable and a Kashmiri. Because he was a Saiyad,[4] there was no limit to his spiritual power. I called him down and asked him to talk to the woman. He went up to her and, reassuring her with a gesture, began to talk in their incomprehensible language. After a few words, the woman's fear disappeared. She came closer to him, burst out sobbing, and wiping her eyes with the corner of her filthy shawl, began to babble away.

Pir Husain explained to me that she was trying to find her husband and had come to Lahore to look for him. He had come here to work some years ago and had not gone home. She had written him a number of letters, but still he had not returned. She had come here to bring him back.

I said, "We'll see about her husband. First, let's get her bundle open." When Pir Husain asked her to, she opened the

[4] A courtesy title for a Muslim of outstanding achievement or noble lineage.

bundle hesitatingly. Inside a piece of cloth there were a couple of dirty rags, and wrapped in some other rags were the remains of maize cakes several days old. There was also an old, Kashmiri-style man's jacket embroidered with flowers and leaves and studded with little round pieces of glass—so crudely done as to be an insult to the art of Kashmir. She unfolded the jacket very reluctantly, as though she didn't want to show it to anyone. Besides this, she had a knife which, after many assurances from Pir Husain, she produced from her inner garments. Why was she carrying a knife? In spite of repeated questioning, she would not say. Turning her face away she said, "For no particular reason."

Here is a Kashmiri woman, who until now has not set foot outside her village, but comes to Lahore alone! She says she is looking for her husband, but she knows no one here and does not know where to look for him. She carries a man's jacket which she tries to keep hidden—and a knife as well. Isn't there something strange about this?

I said to Pir Husain, "She seems to be a very clever woman and it wouldn't surprise me if she is involved in some major crime and has run away. Get the truth out of her."

I turned her over to him and began to work on other matters. From time to time I glanced at her. After quite some time Pir Husain gained her confidence and the woman began to tell her story haltingly. In a short while, she burst out sobbing uncontrollably. Pir Husain tried to comfort her, and in the circumstances, I did not think it proper to intrude. Then Pir Husain came over to me and explained. . . .

This woman lives about thirty miles on the other side of Srinagar, near Bairinag. She covered the 225 miles from there to Jammu on foot, stopping at every station to inquire about her husband, and finally took the Peshawar Express for Lahore. When you ask her where her husband lives, she says Lahore, but she doesn't know his address.

I said, "If she doesn't know his address, where will she find him?—in her head? Either she knows his address or she didn't come here for him."

Pir Husain continued to question her sympathetically for another hour and a half, and here is her story as he understood it.

Thirty years ago, my husband Phajja and some other young men of the village went to Lahore to find work as laborers. At that time I said to him, "Through God's grace, we have plenty here. Eight to ten buffaloes, ten to twelve *ghūmā*[5] of land, apple, walnut and mulberry trees. If we work hard, we can make enough for our needs." His mother, too, tried to coax him to stay. I was very young then, less than twenty. He lost his temper and told me to shut up and said that in seven months, before the flowers blossom on the apple trees, he would be back. He said the streets of Lahore are made of silver. Everyone was going; why shouldn't he?

I cried and cried but he went away. Mother-in-law and I did all the work. We had to plow the fields alone. Mother-in-law would get angry and say, "Better to have had no son than a worthless one like him."

One year went by, then two and three, and every day I cried. When the snow melted, the men who had gone away returned, but my husband did not come back. Two more years passed. Habla's husband, Rahman, came back from Lahore and brought a letter from Phajja with him. It said, "I

---

[5] Roughly 1¼ acres.

have been framed and am in jail. Send some money so I can come home." Mother-in-law and I wept bitterly. We sold two buffaloes and sent him forty rupees. Without telling mother-in-law, I had the post office clerk write a letter for me which said, "You must come soon. Your mother is very unhappy and sick. I cry all the time. I am very frightened. You must come quickly. Mother-in-law is mean to me and says I sent you away, that you went away because you quarreled with me. Now we cannot work alone. Your mother is worn out and without you we are in trouble."

I asked, "Did you get a receipt for the money and an answer to your letter?"

She replied, "The receipt for the money came, but there was no answer to my letter." Trusting in me, she produced three receipts from the pocket of the man's jacket. The first one was stamped October 1906, Bhati Gate, Lahore Post Office. That was the money order for forty rupees. On the back was a thumbprint and scribbled next to it 'Phajja' in Urdu. It also bore the signature of a witness. After showing me the receipts, she continued her story . . .

Year followed year this way. Phajja did not come back. People who went to Lahore and Amritsar to work would bring news of Phajja from time to time. Sometimes I would hear that he was in the hands of the police, sometimes that he had got a job, sometimes that he was a shopkeeper and had become rich. Mother-in-law got sick and died. I was all alone.

Pharu, who had married later than I, had two young, strong sons, and a daughter to do the household chores. Havla's two daughters each had a child. Mamchu's wife died, but he had a sturdy son and a daughter too.

Nine years later, a man brought me a letter from Lahore

saying, "I am sick. I have no money. I am in deep trouble!
Send some money somehow, and I will come right away." I
sold another buffalo and two walnut trees at half price to
Pagsu, and again took forty rupees to the post office clerk to
send and had him write a letter for me, saying, "I am all alone
now. Your mother is dead. Everyone in the village is my
enemy. What is a woman without a husband? This one steals
the harvest; that one steals the walnuts. Hala has stolen all
the silkworms from the mulberry tree. Everyone has several
children. They come and go; they work. But I have no one.
Now I am afraid. I feel beaten. I don't need your money, only
come, please just come."

This time he answered. "Don't be upset. I will start a
business in Lahore and you will come here too. It is very
comfortable here. I will have ornaments made for you." I had
a letter written to him again to come home. It is proper to live
at home. One cannot grow roots in alien places. The fields
and cattle have suffered, but when he came home, everything
would be all right. I was still young, my limbs were still
strong. He would have sons and all would be well. . . .

But no one came and no letter came.

I got sick a lot. There was no one in the house, but
Mamchu would bring water for me and milk the buffaloes.
Another six years passed this way and Mamchu finally said,
"Look, you're getting older. When you were young, your body
was supple and you danced through the day's work. In another five or six years your bones will be stiff. Then what?
Marry me. I have a son. He will look after both of us. Then
you, too, will have a family. Isn't that better? What do you
say?" I began to cry . . . (Now she started crying again.)

I said, "No. Phajja is my husband. When he comes, I will have a family. He will be home soon."

Three years later Phajja wrote saying he could not pay his debts to another moneylender and had been thrown into prison. "Send thirty rupees and I will come home immediately." Now I had to mortgage a *ghūmā* of land and sent the money with a letter saying, "Everything is going to pieces without you. You have spent your whole life away from home. Come back and have a family. Other people's children are grown up already and working, while I am only getting old."

No one came. No letter came. Then I heard he had married again. I wrote him, "You have done a bad thing. All right —call it 'good.' Come back and bring her with you. I will wait on both of you. Just give me a piece of bread twice a day. No matter what—come." No one came.

I was worn out. I couldn't tend the cattle or work in the fields. What was I to do? I was at the end of my rope. I have come to bring him back, that man at whose hands I have endured so much. When I find him, I will ask him, "Why didn't you come home? All we own has gone to ruin. Just come—that's all I ask. It's true we have no children, but we'll have each other for the years that are left. Whoever dies first will have someone to bury him." And she started sobbing.

Reflecting upon the cruel joke Fate had played on her, I asked, "Is that Phajja's jacket?" She nodded yes. After all his deceit, she still held on to that jacket. Perhaps she envisioned the rapture of bringing him back dressed as a bridegroom.

I asked, "Whose knife is that?"

Wiping her eyes, she said, "Mine."

I asked her what she had planned to do with it. She did not answer.

Then Pir Husain repeated my question gently. She replied heatedly, "He destroyed my life. I did everything for him. Because of him I was childless. If he does not come back with me now, I'll cut his throat."

I shivered, but I couldn't be angry or blame her. A person who clearly states her intention to murder someone while sitting in a police station . . . ! Pir Husain picked up the knife and locked it in the safe.

The search for Phajja was on. We checked through the Register of Number 10 [6] criminals. There were all kinds of Phajjas in it—Phajja, Phaiju, Phajlu, Phajle Khan . . . which one of them was Raphiya's Phajja? We asked her to describe him. She said, "He is very good-looking, young, with a lovely beard and mustache . . . and a scar on his right nostril." Scar on right nostril—here he was on the Register— Phajja of Hiramandi. We found him in Lahore's Central Jail where he was being held because he could not post bail. But Raphiya was not to be told about this.

Shah Sahib was approached and his permission obtained, and Miya Yakub Husain had bond posted for Phajja. He took Phajja aside, scolded him properly and got him ready to go home to live a life of ease.

Then they brought him and stood him before Raphiya. Neither recognized the other. When Pir Husain introduced them, Raphiya just stood there motionless, staring—it seemed

[6] The Number 10 Register lists notorious or habitual criminals.

for an eternity—unable to say a word. Doubtless, Raphiya still had in her mind the image of strong, young, twenty-three-year-old Phajja. That withered, white-haired, toothless Phajja with the vacant stare—that could not be her Phajja for whom she had sacrificed her entire life! A deep sigh escaped her, then wordlessly shaking her head, she crept into a corner, hid her face in her shawl and wept—for how long I do not know. No one dared to say anything.

That evening Pir Husain tried to persuade her to take Phajja back. Her eyes flashed and she hissed, "That cheat, that deceiver, that scum! He dragged me through the dirt. I won't even look at him." Leaving his jacket there, she picked up her shawl and walked out in the direction of the railway station.

This was not the moment for words, but the thought came to me. . . . so this is what love is made of, a love that lived for thirty years.

TO UPHOLD RIGHTEOUSNESS

This short story exemplifies Yashpal's total repudiation of ancient Hindu ideals as a basis for twentieth-century life. It represents, as well, rejection of the teaching of his own early life. Yashpal's mother was an ardent believer in the Arya Samaj movement and enrolled him in the gurukul at Hardwar when he was seven years old. He lived there for seven years. A description of this system of education and the gurukul he attended appears in Indian Nationalism and Hindu Social Reform:

> *In 1902 Mahatma Munshi Ram, the leader of the conservative Arya Samajists, founded the famous Gurukula at Hardwar, near the source of the Ganges. Generally regarded as an extraordinary experiment in education, the Gurukula flourished, and similar institutions were established elsewhere. Though its specialty was the training of Sanskrit scholars, and though it was not affiliated with any University, courses included English language and literature, modern sciences, history, and social science; classes were conducted in Hindi, and a degree equivalent to a B.A. was offered. Boys only were admitted—other gurukulas were established for girls—at ages six to eight, on condition that their parents would not have them married before they had completed their course of study at the age of twenty-five. A high degree of physical fitness and discipline was required of the students, in line with Dayananda's admonition that the Hindu 'race' lacked vigor*

*and courage; one Indian visitor found the boys bathing in
the icy waters of the Ganges at 4:30 A.M. when he visited
the place in 1913. No women could distract the students
by their presence in the Gurukula, and vegetarianism was
enforced.*[1]

Yashpal left the gurukul when he was fourteen years old only
because he was too ill to continue his education there. His leaving
for the "real world" at that age was important to his development.
He joined the Congress movement as a volunteer while still in
high school and was disillusioned with its methods and accom-
plishments by the time he entered college. In college he was influenced by the writings of Marx, Lenin and other revolutionaries
and by the success of the Russian Revolution. He concluded that
nothing short of a revolution that would revamp the country's
economic and social structure as well as achieve freedom from
British rule would bring relief to the people of India.

The Arya Samaj ideal of recreating an ancient Hindu kingdom
based on the Vedas he saw not only as foolish but harmful. The
gurukul system of education he saw as not merely irrelevant, but,
as in Gyanvati's case, destructive. Professor Brahmbrat personified
for him much that was backward and unrealistic in Indian society.
Viewing the Hindu ideal of brahmacharya as unnatural, he
demonstrated the evil which could come from it.

The importance of this story is its insights into Yashpal's reaction to his background and the education he received as a child in
gurukul, his rejection of the Arya Samaj approach to Indian problems, and his scorn for the idealization of brahmacharya which he
regards as a denial of normal instincts, and therefore more likely
to lead to moral disaster than to spiritual elevation.

[1] Charles H. Heimsath, *Indian Nationalism and Hindu Social Reform*,
Princeton: Princeton University Press, 1964, pages 296–7.

I N those days when Professor Brahmbrat received his Master of Science degree, very few people had achieved such success. He could have been a professor in a government college or a top government official if he chose, but he did not even consider it. Brahmbrat joined the Ved Prachar Sabha [1]

[1] The Ved Prachar Sabha is a society established by the Arya Samaj for the purpose of teaching the Vedas. The Vedas are a collection of scriptures which provides the basis for Hinduism. They were composed by the priestly class of the Aryas—the people who emigrated into India from the West about the second millenium before Christ. There are four Vedas— the Rig, Yajur, Sama and Atharva. The *Rig Veda,* composed of about 1,000 hymns, is considered the most important.

The Arya Samaj was established by Swami Dayanand Saraswati in 1885 as a society to promote religious and social reform in India. Swami Dayanand had a mystical religious experience when he was a young man which caused him to leave his home and wander through India as a sannyasi (religious mendicant) for fifteen years seeking the truth. The "truth" he found was that the four Vedas contained all the wisdom of the world, and that the later scriptures of Hinduism (Puranas, etc.) led to the corruption of Hindu society. Swami Dayanand pointed out that the existing social evils of India—untouchability, child marriage, the subjection of women to men—did not exist in Vedic times and these practices did not derive authority from the Vedas. He believed that in order to purify Hinduism it was necessary to return to the Vedas, and that the teachings of the Vedas, which heretofore had been the exclusive preserve of Brahmans, should be available to all. To this end gurukuls (schools) were established patterned after ancient Indian ideals. The student (brahmachari) lived at the school, lived austerely and was celibate. This combination of celibacy and austerity (brahmacharya) was in conas a life member and dedicated himself to serving the world by propagating Vedic knowledge. He took the hard vow to impart Vedic wisdom and instruction to the country for his whole life at a salary of 75 rupees a month.

Brahmbrat had studied Western chemistry, but he guarded against the fallacious reasoning which this kind of education produces. It was his indestructible belief that the basic source of all true knowledge is God. The source of all true learning and a treasury of basic knowledge are the Vedas. The hope of furthering world progress based on Western material knowledge seemed to him a vain delusion, just like a mouse who, having come upon a piece of dried ginger, thinks he has discovered a grocery shop.

Brahmbrat often quoted the famous scientist Newton as saying: "When we pick up a beautiful, shining seashell which has floated to the shore from the sea, we are overjoyed. We do not know what a wealth of precious jewels there are in

---

formity with Hindu ideals expressed in the Vedas of appropriate conduct during the period of student life.

When the stage of student life was over, he then passed to the next stage, that of a householder, which involved marriage and the pursuit of worldly pleasures. The period of brahmacharya was completed for most people when student life was over. However, for those who chose to attain a higher level of spiritual life than was sought by the ordinary person, continuation of brahmacharya (asceticism) added to the store of spiritual strength. Asceticism is highly valued in the Hindu religion. In fact, the ancient literature abounds with examples of those who sought and achieved power through the practice of asceticism.

The term brahmacharya is used in this story in two ways: one use applies to the student stage of life. A student is a brahmachari; therefore, he practices brahmacharya as proper conduct for his age and occupation. In another context, brahmacharya is the practice of asceticism, and most particularly, celibacy. Where the term is used in the story, the meaning intended is clear in context.

God's Eternal and Boundless Sea of Powers. We could not
find those precious jewels if He did not grant us His Knowledge and His Grace." Professor Brahmbrat would offer proof
of the insubstantiality of Western science as compared with
the solid logic of Vedic knowledge and the immutability of
the law of cause and effect. He believed that India's subjection to a foreign power, its poverty and misery were the result
of having turned its face away from the wisdom of the Vedas.
In those days when this country, through its power of brahmacharya, was the master of Vedic knowledge, then. . . .

> This country produced the first teachers in the world.
> The world learned morality and religion from the
> people of this country.

Brahmbrat often quoted this Sanskrit shloka [2] in his speeches
as proof of the knowledge gained through the power of brahmacharya in ancient India.

When Professor Brahmbrat was born, the purohit [3] who
suggested the infant's name according to the astrological
signs, must have had a rather romantic nature. The infant
was named Radharaman.[4] When Radharaman was study-

[2] Verse with a meter of eight syllables to the quarter.
[3] Family priest
[4] Lover of Radha; name of Lord Krishna. Radha is a Hindu goddess, the
mistress of Lord Krishna. Their amorous exploits are described in full and
physical detail in *Gitā Govinda,* a Sanskrit poem written by Jayadeva in
the 12th century. At one level the poem is a description of longing and
passion. However, to the followers of the Krishna cult, the poem represents
the desire of the soul (Radha) for union with God (Krishna).

ing at the Anglo-Vedic College in Lahore, he realized that abrahmacharya [5] led to a man's downfall, and that brahmacharya was the path to power. He banished all signs of self-indulgence from his life, and furthermore renounced his obscene name which referred to his improper relations with Mother Radha, and adopted the name of Brahmbrat.[6] He wrote on the wall of his room in the boarding house in large letters:

> OM
> By practicing austerities the gods have attained immortality. Brahmacharya alone is life.[7]

Unlike the other students at school, Brahmbrat did not oil his hair or wear it in shoulder-length ringlets. One saw only the sturdy topknot standing up on the closely-cropped head. Coat buttoned to the neck, pyjama [8] neither tight nor loose and village-made shoes. He did not alter his type of dress after he received his M. Sc. degree nor even when he became a professor. Parents, troubled by youthful attraction to luxury and excessive spending, praised Brahmbrat's simple living and cited him as an example for the young to follow.

His own parents, unaware of the importance of brahmacharya, and ensnared by degenerate social customs, committed the blunder of getting the boy married when he was studying for his entrance exams. Brahmbrat, knowing the value of brahmacharya decided that during college vacation he would

---

[5] Non-celibacy and self-indulgence
[6] Brahmbrat = dedicated to God
[7] OM is a sacred syllable, the uttering of which is thought to have magic properties. It also may stand for God.
[8] trousers

go to his house in the town and his wife would stay at her parents' house. The mute young bride could not comprehend the importance and purpose of her husband's sublime goal, but she could not say anything. However, to Brahmbrat's parents and the parents of the bride, this outrageous behavior by the boy, who had clearly been spoiled in the city atmosphere, was intolerable. The neighbors and relatives interpreted this in various ways: The boy doesn't like his wife . . . He wanted to marry someone else in the city . . . etc. etc. Brahmbrat had to yield to the majority who supported the retrograde customs of society, and, as is written in the Shastras,[9] this too had its consequences. While Brahmbrat was still studying for his Bachelor of Science degree and writing essays in the school newspaper on the maintenance of brahmacharya, a letter arrived informing him that he had just become the father of a beautiful little girl. The news of the child, proof of the violation of his vow, filled him with anguish and contempt for himself. To atone for his sin, he resolved that he would not have sexual intercourse with his wife for twelve years. That strength which God had given him to spread His Message, he would not destroy that way!

Lahore was the center of Western education in the Punjab. Professor Brahmbrat was convinced that it was impossible to pursue the ideal of brahmacharya in the luxurious and sinful atmosphere of that city. He agreed to manage the Anglo-Vedic High School in a small town on the bank of the Vyas River. He felt that boys raised in relatively simple and health-

[9] Hindu scriptures dealing with religious and civil law and practice.

ful surroundings away from the city, given proper Vedic instruction, could be made worthy to disseminate throughout the world the Vedic knowledge which had been transmitted through the rishis.[10] Fulfillment of the sacred mission of the Aryas—to convert the whole world to the Aryan faith—cannot be achieved by city boys who dress their curls with perfumed oil, whose skin is yellow-stained by cigarettes, and who have turned their faces away from Nature. Village boys —their strength drawn from the lap of Mother Nature, healthy, protected against the destructive effects of sex, luxury and sin—only they could succeed in this goal.

Professor Brahmbrat established a Brahmachari Boarding House near the Anglo-Vedic School two miles from town on the bank of the river. The boarding house students were not permitted to go to the city or the bazaar. The professor had a high wall built surrounding the house, with pieces of broken glass on top. The diet and clothing of the boys and all the things they used conformed to the precepts of brahmacharya. Brahmbrat himself kept a sharp lookout so that no evil influence could enter the place. Every evening he would lecture to the boys: "God has given us this beautiful body and good health so that we may carry out His Laws and His Aims. By the practice of brahmacharya the body and mind grow strong. Abrahmacharya destroys both body and mind."

He instructed them to get up before daybreak, move their bowels, bathe and exercise. He explained that cold showers were essential to brahmacharya. "The moment any evil thought comes to your mind, recite the Gayatri mantra.[11]

---

[10] Sages of ancient times; the composers of the Vedic hymns.
[11] The Gayatri mantra is a verse from a hymn of the *Rig Veda* addressed to the solar god Savitṛ. The verse in translation:

Smoking, tart foods, spicy foods and very sweet foods are all harmful to brahmacharya. Lewd songs and pictures are inimical to brahmacharya . . ." When he discovered lapses of this kind, he would flog the culprits and lecture to them that such activities are destructive of brahmacharya and such destruction is suicidal.

Hearing praise of brahmacharya and censure of abrahmacharya over and over again roused the curiosity of the young boys. What is abrahmacharya? What happens when you commit abrahmacharya? They felt a great urge to eat tart and spicy foods and to refrain from taking cold showers, and it gave them pleasure to feel that they had in this way demonstrated the courage to violate brahmacharya. But the more sophisticated boys told the others knowingly, "The real abrahmacharya is in the relations between boys and girls and men and women."

Having had these evil thoughts before they came, these boys indulged in bad acts of abrahmacharya several times. Professor Brahmbrat beat them for their crimes and turned them out of the boarding hosue as a lesson to the others. For a long time afterward, the other pupils would compare ideas and speculate about these crimes.

On behalf of society and the world Professor Brahmbrat went to war against ignorance, bad habits and self-indulgence. He held a tight rein on himself in order to maintain his own brahmacharya and he required the same of his students. He

---

> "Let us think on the lovely splendour
> Of the god Savitṛ,
> That he may inspire our minds."

(From A. L. Basham, *The Wonder that Was India*, New York: Grove Press, 1954, p. 162)

used to preach to them: "The pure bliss and peace which we experience in carrying out God's work can be achieved only with the strength we acquire through brahmacharya and self-restraint. What can you accomplish if you ruin that God-given body with sin? The pleasure that comes from sin is like the taste of pepper. Nature tells us to stay away from it. The pepper burns our tongue, but we, persisting in our own ruin, become accustomed to it. In the same way, whenever we perform an evil deed, God puts shame and fear in our hearts. This is a warning to us from God. We should recognize His warning. Happiness, strength and peace come from obeying God's will. . . ."

Professor Brahmbrat was held in high esteem by society for his teaching and his conduct.

Professor Brahmbrat stood firm on his twelve-year vow of brahmacharya, but when his daughter entered her sixth year, he became concerned about her education. He had named her Gyanvati.[12] If he brought the child and her mother to live with him, he would be putting his remaining six years of brahmacharya in peril. The Omniscient God, in His boundless and incomprehensible design, gave Brahmbrat a helping hand in this difficult problem. For Gyanvati's mother, her appointed task completed, her time on earth came to an end. To remove every obstacle from the path of her husband's worthy goal, she returned to the lap of God.

Brahmbrat took Gyanvati away from the grandparents' corrupting influence and permissive environment. Gyanvati's

----

[12] Gyanvati = one who has knowledge

mother and grandmother had adorned the tiny wrists with
gold bracelets. They had painted her little hands with henna
and braided her dust-filled hair.

Gyanvati's father stripped all this slovenliness from her body
with loving persuasion and firm authority. He had her hair
cut like a boy. He taught her to say namaste [13] and recite the
Gayatri mantra. He taught her hymns in praise of God. He
addressed her as "Son Gyan." When guests came, she recited
the Gayatri mantra with perfect intonation. When her father
asked her, "What will you be?" she answered, "A
brahmacharini." [14] After she ate or belched or hiccuped, she
said, "Om."

It was difficult without a wife to make proper arrangements
for the little girl at home, so Brahmbrat, obeying the injunc-
tions of the rishis, entered her in a gurukul for girls. For
twelve years Gyanvati led a well-ordered life. To protect his
daughter from bad influences, the professor did not take her
out of the gurukul even at vacation time. Gyanvati completed
her twelve years of education. She gained a thorough knowledge of Sanskrit and Vedic literature. She could expound on
the *Mahābhāṣya* [15] and *Nirukta*.[16] Her body was thin and
brittle from the rigorous life in the gurukul, but she was
healthy. She seemed as unaware of the demands of her young
body as an ascetic. She looked bewildered by her attempts to
understand her own feelings and the world.

Two months had gone by already since Gyanvati had come

[13] Polite form of greeting
[14] A female ascetic
[15] Patanjali's commentary on Panini's Sanskrit grammar
[16] Oldest exegetical work on the *Rig Veda*

home. Her father's house, which was next to the boarding
house, was composed of three rooms. One was used as a school
office and storage place for books. In another room there was a
wooden bed where the father slept. When Gyanvati came, a
charpoy was put in the third room for her since a wooden bed
could not be made immediately. The professor's servant, Motiram, slept in the kitchen or on the veranda. Motiram had
lived with the professor since childhood and learned Hindi.
He had read the *Ramayana,*[17] the *Mahabharata,*[18] and other
books. And finally there was a cow, Kamala. If Kamala gave
her pure milk in great quantity, the professor and the servant
both drank it. If not, then only the professor.

When Gyanvati joined the family, Kamala had been giving
milk for a year. Her calf, Ketu, was an unwanted nuisance
and had been sent away. Kamala gave less milk. When the
professor noticed how thin Gyanvati was because of her aus-
tere life, he ordered Motiram to buy a seer [19] of milk every
day. It gave Gyanvati greater pleasure to take care of Kamala
than to get more milk. Until then Kamala had seen only men
in that house, but now that there was one of her own kind,
she was overjoyed. She would look up at Gyanvati, big-eyed
and loving and moo tenderly and affectionately. Gyanvati
enjoyed stroking her soft, smooth back and rubbing her neck.
She liked to put her arms around the cow's neck. She had
never felt the touch of living skin before. She learned from

---

[17] One of the two great epics of India, describing the exploits of King
Rama (Krishna in human form) who overcame the demon Ravana.

[18] The other great Indian epic which tells of the struggle between the
Kauravas and the Pandavas.

[19] Slightly over two pounds

Motiram how to milk the cow. Although Motiram was a servant, he was a young man too, and different from the girls she had always played with.

Since Gyanvati had completed her period of brahmacharya she was now entitled to eat tart and spicy foods and she enjoyed their flavor. These stimulating substances were left out of the professor's food. Motiram prepared their meals separately. Seeing Gyanvati's enjoyment of flavor, he was not stingy. One gets pleasure from giving satisfaction to others.

Motiram had learned to read and write Hindi. He borrowed books occasionally from the pandit in the Arya Samaj temple or from the schoolteacher in order to pass the time and because he enjoyed reading. There was not only *The Life of Swami Dayanand* and *The Life of Hanumanji,* but also *Chandrakanta Santati* [20] and other worldly novels and mystery stories. Gyanvati, all alone at home, had nothing else to do. She enjoyed those books like a person who, after a lifetime of following a strict diet under doctor's orders, suddenly is allowed to eat all the previously prohibited foods. The appeal of the Commentaries on the Vedas and Upanishads and the Annual Reports of the Ved Prachar Sabha could not last forever.

When the professor had sent the little six-year-old Gyan to gurukul to be educated, she was like a little toy that could say namaste and recite the Gayatri mantra. When she returned at eighteen, she was still his daughter, but a young woman too. She was the image of that young woman who, eighteen years before, had overwhelmed Brahmbrat when he came home

[20] Hindi detective story

from college, had given birth to Gyanvati, and was the reason for his twelve-year vow of celibacy. The sight of Gyanvati brought back the memory of her mother to Brahmbrat. The girl was just like her in form and coloring, but her conduct was quite different. The mother had been a village girl—shy and shrinking. The daughter, by the right of education, was high spirited and lively.

Unaccustomed to the society of a woman, the professor felt ill at ease with Gyanvati. He avoided looking at her. To hold fast to his vow of brahmacharya, he followed these rules: Wherever possible, he avoided any contact with women. If he had to be in the presence of a woman, he addressed her as Mother or Sister.

He could hardly call Gyanvati Mother or Sister, but he felt it would be hypocritical to call her Daughter, as though he were suddenly pretending to be an old man. He was only thirty-eight years old, and as a result of his disciplined life, the hair on his head was still black.

When Gyanvati came home a grown young woman, his Arya Samaj friends pointed out to him that he ought to give some thought to her marriage. The professor himself was concerned about finding a desirable husband for his daughter. He was considering some gurukul graduates and some worthwhile teachers. He did not have the courage to speak to his young daughter of marriage—that girl who had never been exposed to sex or the atmosphere of a household. The professor began to think that perhaps she ought to take a vow of brahmacharya and carry on the work of teaching the Vedas. At such times, he would reflect on how simple everything would have been if Gyanvati had been a boy. Then he would reproach himself for questioning the design and dispensation of the Immutable, transcendent and eternal Brahma.[21] God had made man and woman alike to bring to light the knowledge of Himself. In both men and women there was the fullness of the knowledge of Brahma. The son and daughter of Ashoka, Mahendra and Mahendri,[22] both went forth to propagate the faith.

He grew angry with himself because his mind was constantly turning to thoughts of women. He explained to himself logically, "It strengthens one to suppress evil thoughts. Thinking about women leads to desire. That is the worst enemy of knowledge. The thing to fear is unawareness of the attraction of desire . . ."

When his young daughter came home, he thought of asking his old, almost forgotten aunt to come and live in the house. He began to spend most of his time in the office at school so that the young students and teachers would not have any reason to be around the house.

The Ved Prachar Sabha was meeting on Sunday at noon in Lahore. Professor Brahmbrat had to attend. He took the early morning train to Lahore.

It was noon. Motiram was in the bazaar, shopping. Gyanvati was lying on the charpoy, reading. In the backyard Kamala was mooing loudly. Gyanvati was absorbed in the book, but when the mooing persisted, she began to feel sorry for the

[21] God
[22] Ashoka was a famous Indian emperor (273–236 B.C.) who embraced Buddhism. According to legend, Mahendra is credited with converting the people of Ceylon to Buddhism.

cow and very annoyed at Motiram. . . . He is very bad. He probably hasn't fed the cow. . . . She put her book down, got a basketful of straw and dropped it into the cow's feeding trough. Kamala did not look at the food. She mooed louder and grew very agitated. Gyanvati looked at Kamala anxiously. She surmised the cow was thirsty and brought her a bucket of water. She made kissing sounds to comfort her. Kamala saw the water, shook her head hard, and mooed again. She kept circling the peg, pulling at the rope and trying to break it. Gyanvati, upset by the cow's distress, petted her and asked, "Kamala, what is it? What's the matter? What do you want?"

Motiram returned. Gyanvati anxiously described Kamala's behavior to him. Motiram looked at Kamala and said calmly, "The cow has to go out. Bibiji, give me a rupee."

"Where?" Gyanvati asked with concern, "to the animal hospital?"

"No. To the bull," Motiram laughed at Gyanvati's ignorance.

"Oh, why?" Gyanvati gasped in astonishment.

"Doesn't the cow have to go to the bull?"

"What for?" Gyanvati insisted. That problem had never presented itself to her in gurukul. She had not read anything about it in a book.

"Please give me a rupee," Motiram said. The professor always made Motiram account for each paisa.[23] Gyanvati, too, asked him why he wanted a rupee.

"The owner of the bull charges for it," Motiram said.

"For what?" asked Gyanvati.

"The cow will be cured. She will be all right."

[23] One-hundredth of a rupee.

"How will she be cured?"

"When I come back, I'll tell you."

Gyanvati took a five-rupee note out of her father's wardrobe and gave it to Motiram. Motiram led the cow out by the rope. Gyanvati paced the rooms nervously, then lay down on the charpoy. Her heart was heavy with concern for the cow.

Motiram returned at sunset with the cow. Kamala was completely serene. Gyanvati looked at her and said to Motiram, "Now tell me what was the matter."

Motiram smiled, "Don't you know? The cow goes to the bull."

"Oh, poor Kamala," Gyanvati's eyes were wide with dismay. She sighed deeply and asked, "Didn't the bull hurt her? Tell me exactly what happened."

Motiram wanted to change the subject, and he started to go into the kitchen, but Gyanvati insisted on an answer. Her persistence excited Motiram. His eyes reddened and his speech became thick. "It's like men and women do," he said.

Gyanvati's curiosity was boundless. She asked, "How? What do they do?" And she asked him again.

Motiram explained in one short sentence.

When Gyanvati suddenly understood, sweat poured out of every pore of her body. She reprimanded him, "Nonsense. The cow is a very gentle and holy animal. That is a very bad thing."

Motiram was so aroused he could no longer control himself. He seized Gyanvati's elbow saying, "Come on. I'll show you." Gyanvati protested against being held like that, but she was not angry. And the nature of her protest was such that it excited Motiram even more. As Motiram held her close to

him, Gyanvati stammered, "No, this is wrong." Motiram persuaded her, "See what it's like just this once. Why is it
wrong? Shri Ramchandraji, Sita and Shri Krishna [24] have all
done it." When Gyanvati reminded him how angry her father
would be, Motiram said, "He's in Lahore. He won't be back
until tomorrow." Gyanvati saw that Motiram was not listen-
ing to her, and she was not inclined to resist. Her head spun
and her protests grew weaker. She was afraid of committing a
sin, but her mind countered with, "I have completed my
period of brahmacharya. In the days of the rishis and the
munis, [25] a girl chose her own husband. Brahmacaryīn tapasā
kanyā vindate yuvānaṃ patim. . . ." [26] Before she allowed
herself to be overwhelmed by Motiram's passion, while still
conscious of her responsibility, she held his eager hands in her
limp hands and said, "Quickly, recite the marriage mantra.
. . . Om Viṣṇuryoni kalpabatu tvaṣṭā. . . ." [27]

[24] Shri Ramchandra is Rama, the husband of Sita, and the hero of the
Ramayana. Krishna is the Lord Krishna referred to earlier as the lover of
Radha.

[25] Holy men mentioned in *Rig Veda*

[26] Gyanvati is reciting a line in Sanskrit from a hymn in the *Atharva-
Veda*, XI, 5, 18. The sentence translates: Through brahmacharya a maiden
finds a young husband. (de Bary, *Sources of Indian Tradition,* Page 19).
(See also F. Max Müller, *Sacred Books of the East,* Vol. XLII, Page 217).

[27] The portion of the Sanskrit mantra which Yashpal quotes above is
puzzling for several reasons: First, the mantra quoted is not part of the
marriage mantra, but rather a portion of a conception (*Garbhādhān*)
mantra. Second, the Sanskrit appears to be misprinted (see below). Third,
it seems unlikely that Gyanvati would recite this mantra since it is addressed to the female, and presumably therefore Motiram would say it.
However, later in the story, Gyanvati tells her father that she recited the
Garbhādhān mantra.

There are several versions of the conception mantra. The one in the
standard references that appears closest to the version quoted by Yashpal is

They forgot all about cooking and eating. They forgot to shut the door against thieves in the night.

The professor had gone to Lahore by the early morning train. From noon until four o'clock he was at the meeting. He started worrying about the young girl alone at home, and that thought compelled him to return. He took the evening train, arriving at the station at nine o'clock at night. He started walking home by the narrow footpath through the fields, a heavy stick in his hand and a bundle of papers under his arm. It had turned cool, and since it was the eve of the full moon of Phagun,[28] moonlight shone everywhere as bright as day. Caressed by the gentle breeze, the golden sheaves of wheat rippled all the way to the river's edge. A sandpiper at the bank of the river called out in a piercing voice, accenting the silent, peaceful beauty of the moonlit night. The path to home was three miles long.

from the Brihadāraṇyaka Upanishad, *Sacred Books of the East,* Volume XV, Part II, Page 221, Lines 3, 4. Conforming the transliteration to the story, and quoting only that portion which is relevant, the mantra is as follows:

". . . Viṣṇur yoniṃ kalpayatu, Tvaṣṭā. . . ."

One translation of the conception mantra from the Grihya-Sūtra of Hiraṇyakeshin, *Sacred Books of the East,* Volume XXX, Part II, Page 199 (with transliteration of names conformed to above) follows:

"May Viṣṇu make thy womb ready; may Tvaṣṭṛ frame the shape
(of the child);

May Prajāpati pour forth (the sperm); may Dhatṛ give
thee conception."

Compare this also with Ralph T. H. Griffith, *Hymns of the Ṛgveda,* Vol. II, Book X, Hymn 184:1, P. 613.

[28] Phagun is the last month of the Hindu calendar, corresponding to February–March.

Ideas about the young girl's future continually intruded on his thoughts. "What if she decided, at her age, to preach Vedic doctrine? When she speaks from the platform about brahmacharya and knowledge, the sophisticated young men will look her over from head to toe, at her hair, at her round and rising bosom. Even if she taught only women, she would still have contact with men. She has never been exposed to sensuality and desire; therefore, for the moment, her brahmacharya has been maintained. The world is filled with sensualists and temptation, and a person has to be very strong to protect himself. That strength is achieved only through the constant exercise of self-discipline. It has taken so much effort for me to acquire this strength! At every step in life I have been tested. How hard it is to keep the vow of brahmacharya!"

His thoughts led to his memory of that time when he was twenty when. . . . "This girl was the result of it . . . and after that, how much discipline it has taken to suppress my desire . . . but is it possible for everyone?"

From this memory the professor was led to another— "Gyanvati's mother, Lajo, was just like Gyanvati is now. She was a powerful river of sex. . . . I can still smell the fragrance of coriander oil on her smooth and carefully braided hair . . . It was on a moonlit night just like this in autumn on the roof of the house. . . . Gyanvati is taller than Lajo. . . . Lajo used to stoop a little as she walked, but Gyanvati is straight. . . . Gyanvati's breasts are more. . . ." The professor stumbled against a bush and nearly fell. At that moment the sharp cry of the sandpiper sent a warning to him. The professor was jolted to his senses. He realized that his blood was racing and his body was hot. He controlled his breathing by pranayam [29] until the excitement of his body subsided. He recited the Gayatri mantra and upbraided himself, "She is your daughter! All the young women in the world are your daughters, sisters and mother!" And he began to think how hard it was to maintain brahmacharya. "How many thoughts like thieves come to rob a man of his priceless jewel of brahmacharya! . . . With a body like that, is it possible for Gyanvati . . . ?"

The professor warned himself again, "I must not allow myself to think about a woman's body." To gain mastery over his mind he recited the Gayatri mantra over and over.

Seeing the doors of the house open at that hour, the professor was incensed at the carelessness of the servant and his daughter. There was no light inside either. What was going on? Weren't they there? With things left like that, any thief could get into the house.

He went inside without calling out. From his room he entered Gyanvati's room and saw her lying with the servant on the charpoy. He lifted his stick.

Motiram, hearing a noise, stood up and felt the blow of the stick on his shoulder. He ran away, out the door and through the courtyard. The next blow of the stick struck Gyanvati. She lifted her arms to protect herself, but she did not utter a word. The professor threw the stick down. He bent over Gyanvati, lying on the charpoy, her clothes disarrayed, and beat her and slapped her. His hands hit her everywhere. The touch of her body excited him. He remembered a short time ago walking on the footpath comparing Gyanvati's breasts to Lajo's breasts. His mind, blinded by anger, saw the scene of

[29] Breath control; used as a part of yogic discipline

eighteen years before. His hands no longer beat Gyanvati—they were petting and stroking and holding her.

Gyanvati had endured her father's beating without a word, but now she tried to hold his unrestrained hands. She protested, "Father, what are you doing?"

The professor lost all reason. He slammed his hand on her mouth to prevent her from calling out and tried with all his strength to overcome her. Gyanvati, horrified, wrenched herself free and hissed, "Father, this is incest! I won't let you commit this sin!"

The professor, furious, lunged at Gyanvati again, raging, "Sinner! Weren't you fornicating with the servant?" Gyanvati, pushing away from the professor spoke up fearlessly, "No! I chose a young man for my husband. I performed the Gārbhādhan mantra."

The professor was absolutely stunned. For a moment he stood speechless staring at Gyanvati. Without a word he left the house. The brilliant moonlight had begun to dim. Hour after hour the professor paced round and round the house. He despised himself—he wanted to break his head open against a rock. "How could I for one moment have lost my head and broken my lifelong vow? What is the use of such a vile and dishonored life? I cannot show my face to society and the world. There is nothing left but to kill myself."

His head down, he started walking toward the bridge on the Vyas River. To jump from the bridge into the water would be an easy way to commit suicide. With that resolution made, he thought as he walked toward the bridge, "My life can no longer be dedicated to my sacred goal. What is left for me but suicide?" To insure the salvation of his soul after death and to maintain a pure and peaceful mind at the time of dying, the professor kept repeating the word OM and the Gayatri mantra. He made a wish that in his next birth he would become a sannyasi and be celibate for his entire life.

When he reached the bridge, the sandpiper again cried out in his harsh voice. By that time, the professor's stormy emotions had subsided and he wondered, "What warning is God giving me now?" Suddenly he remembered the saying of the rishi:

> A suicide goes to that region of Hell
> Which is devoid of the light of the sun.

The professor reasoned, "Sin cannot be washed away by sin. Sin can be expiated only by repentance and austerities." The wind blew colder. The professor sat on the bridge and said to himself, "Why should I sacrifice God's work and my life's goal because I slipped for a moment on to the path of corruption? Associating with a woman is the enemy of achievement. That was the fault of circumstances. Should I become a sannyasi tomorrow? Or can I continue my work and fulfill my need for a family life? No, I would lose the respect of society. I will become a sannyasi."

The professor walked off the bridge to home. He took a cold bath, woke Gyanvati and told her to bathe in cold water too. Then he lit the sacred fire and said to Gyanvati, who was seated before the holy fire of the yagya,[30]

"Yesterday you lost your self-control and committed a sin. A girl can marry and enter married life only when she has the consent of her parents. That is the sin for which I beat you. Today I will become a sannyasi. Everyone should behave

---

[30] Religious ceremony

properly in keeping with his stage in life. I am arranging your marriage to a suitable man. It harms the mind to keep remembering a sin. Take a vow before God that you will never, under any circumstances, mention this incident. Otherwise your life will be ruined by scandal and hardship. An honorable life is the goal of righteousness. You must do what I have told you to uphold righteousness."

THE EMPEROR'S JUSTICE

"The Emperor's Justice" (Shahanshāh kā Nyāy), the tale of the innocent, helpless "little man," who is the victim of the corruption of the qazis and the complacence of the Shah, is a story of universal appeal. Yashpal's inspiration may have been an actual incident in the life of Emperor Jahangir.

It was said of this Emperor, who reigned in India from 1605 to 1627, that he, too, was devoted to justice, so much so that he ordered the setting up of a "chain of justice"

> *to which any supplicant could attach his petition. As he pulled the chain a bell was sounded and the petition was promptly pulled up and provision made for its satisfactory disposal. Once it was said that the bell was sounded during the night and on enquiry, it was discovered that there was no man but only an ass. The benevolent paragon of justice soon summoned its owner and ordered him to provide proper fodder to it on pain of punishment. Thus the Emperor redressed the wrong of even an ass."* [1]

This "chain of justice" was no common rope. Jahangir himself said,

---

[1] A. B. Pandey, *Later Medieval India*, Allahabad: Central Book Depot, 1963, pages 443–4

'I ordered that the chain should be of pure gold, and be thirty gaz [2] long with 60 bells upon it.' [3]

Mahajan estimates that it must have cost the Emperor about three lakhs [4]—in present-day dollars over $60,000.

As it turned out, poor Budhva would have been better off without the Emperor's justice, but authorities on this subject suggest that the administration of justice under the Mughals, even without the intervention of the Emperor, left something to be desired. Apparently the qazis were notoriously corrupt.

> Every provincial capital had its local kazi, who was appointed by the chief kazi; and these appointments were frequently purchased by bribery. Popular dislike and contempt of these exponents of civil law are enshrined in the adage: "When the kazi's bitch died, the whole town was at the funeral: when the kazi himself died, not a soul followed his coffin. [5]

Emperor Jahangir resembles Yashpal's "Asylum of the World" in another important respect. Although the drinking of wine is forbidden to Muslims, Jahangir was a notorious drunkard. One historian has written, in apparent indignation:

> . . . his image may be seen depicted on his coins, wine-cup in hand, with unblushing effrontery . . . [6]

However, Gibbon, as quoted by Edwardes and Garrett, takes a more tolerant view, observing:

> The wines of Shiraz have always prevailed over the law of the Prophet. [7]

[2] A *gaz* is a yard in length.

[3] V. D. Mahajan, *The Muslim Rule in India*, Delhi: S. Chand & Co., 1962, page 103

[4] *Ibid.*

[5] S. M. Edwardes and H. L. O. Garrett, *Mughal Rule in India*, London: Oxford University Press, 1930, page 191

[6] Stanley Lane-Poole, *Medieval India Under Mohammedan Rule* (A.D. 712–1764), Delhi: Universal Book and Stationery Co., 1963, page 212

[7] Edwardes and Garrett, *op. cit.*, page 195

THE Emperor was deeply devoted to justice. The nobles of the court, describing his virtues, would say, "The Asylum of the World [1] is dedicated to justice." Hearing this, the Emperor enjoyed bliss more exquisite than if he were borne away in a trance on waves of gentle music floating in a ship of harmony, and greater ecstasy than mellowing in *shīrāzī* [2] and flying free into the blue sky of his Begam Nureharam's eyes. He felt he set an example of perfection no man could equal, and for his virtue would live on in the memory of his people long after he had departed this world. He would be immortal.

The Emperor, indeed, had a passion for justice, and he resolved to perfect this justice and make it all-embracing. He was determined that no poor person would be deprived of it. Whether his subjects had food or not, justice they must have! To give food is God's work, but to give justice is the duty of the King. God may provide food or He may not, but the King will provide justice!

This good Emperor thought: I have appointed Qazis,[3] Mullas,[4] and Darogas [5] throughout the land to dispense justice in

---

[1] Epithet of Kings.

[2] The wine of the city of Shiraz—now Iran—then Persia.

[3] A Muslim judge or law officer.

[4] A learned Muslim, one who is especially versed in Arabic and Persian literature.

[5] A sub-inspector of police.

my stead, but they are, after all, only human beings. They may be influenced by venality and prejudice, and they may be unfair. It is our duty to protect the people from the injustice of the Qazis, Mullas and Darogas.

The Emperor knew it wasn't easy for the common people to gain the audience of their Ruler. Hundreds of soldiers, rigid and ready, were stationed from the main entrance of the Royal Palace all the way to the Darbar.[6] Their swords drawn, hundreds of eunuchs stood alert at the gates of the harem. Therefore, the King ordered that a large bell be suspended from the window of his Pleasure Room down to the ground.

In the city, the following Proclamation was announced by Royal Command to the roll of drums: By the Decree of God, under the Sovereignty of the Emperor! Let it be known to all from the highest to the low that a Bell has been hung from the window of the Pleasure Room of His Majesty, the Lord of the People, the Asylum of the World. By ringing this Bell, whoever needs justice can present his petition in the presence of the Emperor!

The Emperor's bureaucrats—the Qazis, Mullas and Darogas—were dismayed when they heard the King's Proclamation. They appealed to the Chief Qazi: "If the Asylum of the World, Himself, metes out justice, what will be left for the Qazis, Mullas and Darogas to do?" The Chief Qazi smiled. The mental capacity of his bureaucracy moved him to pity.

He said: "Who has the responsibility to see that the Emperor's Bell of Justice is rung? Whose duty is it to guard this Bell? Obviously, the Emperor's bureaucracy! The Emperor protects the country. Therefore, he is Master of the Country.

[6] Hall of Audience

The Emperor's bureaucracy protects the person of the Emperor and his Bell . . . now, do you understand?"

All the Qazis, Mullas and Darogas bowed their heads in reverent admiration of the Chief Qazi's wisdom and strategy. By the order of the Beneficent Emperor, armed soldiers were appointed to guard the Bell which had been hung for the Call for Justice.

The Emperor waited in his Pleasure Room to hear the ring of the Bell of Justice, while he sipped iced *shīrāzī* and *argbānī* [7] served in crystal goblets by his Begam Nureharam. The Bell of Justice did not call for justice. The realization that there was no injustice in his domain was a source of unending satisfaction to the Beneficent Emperor.

One evening, Budhva the Dhobi [8] and his bullock, loaded with wash, came home from the ghat.[9] Budhva, completely exhausted, slumped down on his cot even before he tied the bullock to its peg. The moment he lay down, he fell asleep. Budhva's bullock, enjoying the full benefit of freedom, set out to wander where his fancy led, until he came to a bazaar. There he stopped before a sweets shop and began to lick on a lump of gur.[10] The shopkeeper, seeing this outrage, gave him his lumps on the back with a lathi,[11] while he rained down curses on the bullock's owner.

The bullock ran on. As he passed the stables of a rich man

---

[7] A kind of wine
[8] Washerman
[9] River bank
[10] Sometimes called jaggery. Hard, brownish, unrefined sugar.
[11] A wooden stick with a metal tip usually used by policemen.

and saw the fresh grass stored for the horses, he could not restrain his tongue from savoring its flavor. The rich man's servants then proceeded to honor the bullock's back with whips and bamboo rods while they showed him the way out.

The bullock rambled on through alleys and bazaars, luxuriating in his freedom, until he reached the Emperor's Palace. There he caught sight of the Bell hanging from the window of the Emperor's Pleasure Room. In the darkness it looked like a lump of gur. He started toward it. The armed guards stationed to watch over the Bell of Justice were dozing nearby. They were protecting the bell from human beings seeking justice—not animals.

Tempted by the "gur," Budhva's bullock rushed at the bell. At the touch of his mouth, it rang out.

The soldiers fell all over one another in confusion, but at the same time, the Palace Official appointed to listen for the clang of the bell, called out: "Who goes there? Who wishes to plead for justice in the presence of the Emperor, the Asylum of the World? Let the petitioner be presented!" Now it was too late to drive the bullock away.

Stupefied with wine, the dedicated Emperor lurched forward, eager to dispense justice. When he saw the petitioner was a bullock, he was quite startled. He rubbed his eyes and looked carefully—yes, it really was a bullock! And then he thought: The beasts of the kingdom are my subjects, too, and they should also enjoy the benefit of justice. The Emperor commanded the bullock: "Present your petition!"

At the animal's silence, the King realized that a bullock cannot speak. Nevertheless, it was his duty to understand the petition of his mute subjects. He rubbed his eyes again, looked intently at the bullock and pondered. He saw the lathi marks on its body. Now he realized why the bullock had called for justice!

The Emperor ordered the Kotwal: [12] "Find the owner of this bullock and bring him here to be tried." Immediately the Kotwal seized Budhva and stood him before His Highness.

Addressing the culprit, the Emperor said: "Your bullock has appealed to Our Presence to be redressed for your cruel beating." Then, turning to the Kotwal, he ordered: "First, count the lashes on this bullock's back, then whip Budhva the Dhobi that number of times in the Town Square."

Budhva trembled at the sentence. Touching his head to the ground, he implored: "Asylum of the World, only with flowers do I wipe my bullock. I have never beaten him. Let any witness come forward and say he has seen me beat my bullock."

The Emperor was shocked at the defendant's presumption in raising objections to his justice, but in the interest of that justice, he tolerated it and said: "Ignorant lout, We are appalled that you dare to question Our justice. A subject who doubts the Emperor's justice is committing the most heinous of crimes. When Our Majesty passes judgment, there is no need for witness or evidence. Our Kotwal has arrested you. We have sentenced you. Therefore, you are guilty." And the Kotwal, executing the Emperor's orders to the letter, led Budhva away in shackles.

When the Lord of the People returned to his Pleasure Room, Begam Nureharam praised him for his promptness in bestowing justice. The Emperor took a newly filled cup of

---

[12] The Chief Officer of Police in a town or city.

wine from her hands and said contentedly, "Begam, today the world has witnessed that under Our Sovereignty, not only human beings but animals also enjoy justice."

Fatigued by his labors in the Court of Justice, but serene in his success, he accepted another cup of wine and drained it at one gulp.

ONE CIGARETTE

Yashpal is not only an effective teller of tales, but an important writer of social protest. "One Cigarette" is an example of his special concern for the inferior position of women in India. Damati, the heroine, is strong, self-respecting and brave. The traditions of society keep her in total dependence upon her in-laws and her husband, and the law upholds tradition. She is victimized by her husband's family, preyed upon by strangers, abandoned by her husband, and treated as a chattel by the law. Custom and law combine to reduce her to helplessness.

When Damati left home to find her husband in the cantonment, she was jailed as a fugitive and kept in prison until he came to identify and claim her. When her husband refused to take her back, then:

> . . . . the government was not willing to let Damati have space in jail. It was the responsibility of the government to deliver the runaway wife to Vajdatt since she was his property. However, when Vajdatt refused to exercise his right to his wife, the government was no longer concerned with her.

Yashpal's compassion for women, a consistent feature of his writing, may well be due to the influence of his mother. He wrote in Sinhāvalokan [1] that if it were not for her determination to educate her children and her willingness to endure great hardships

---

[1] Yashpal, *Sinhāvalokan*, Vol. 1 Page 59

to secure their future, he could have looked forward only to the life of a peddler of goods with a pack on his back or a menial laborer in the city.

To educate her sons, Yashpal's mother left their home in the cool hills of Kangra and came to the hot, dusty plains to work in an Arya Samaj school for girls. She wanted Yashpal to attend a government college to become a lawyer. When he was graduated from high school, he was awarded a scholarship to attend a government college. However, the desire to work for national freedom had already become the governing factor in his life. While in high school he served as a Congress volunteer, going from village to village making speeches on behalf of India's independence. He also served as a volunteer teaching Untouchables to read and write.

Yashpal declined the college scholarship because it seemed more urgent to him to work for India than to seek financial security and professional status. Finally, he agreed to attend National College in Lahore, which had been founded by Lala Lajpat Rai for the purpose of training young men to serve their country. Since no scholarship was available there, his mother gave him her savings of thirty years so that he would continue his education.

At National College, where the Hindustan Socialist Republican Army was formed, Yashpal met Bhagat Singh and Sukhdev. Yashpal learned not law but revolution at the college. However, his mother always honored his right to follow a path completely different from her own without reproach or reminder of his debt to her. Wherever Yashpal mentions his mother in his autobiography, it is to tell of her encouragement and moral support while he was a revolutionary and later a prisoner.

Yashpal paid his debt to his mother, not in the usual way of sons by making her lot easier, but by pressing for social reform, through his writing, on behalf of all the women of India.

D AMATI was a Brahman, but a lower order of Brahman. Lower because her family, despite the fact they were Brahmans, plowed the fields. Their bodies were contaminated by hard work and the soil of the earth. Constant association with soil and filth had defiled their conduct and speech as well. Their prestige and esteem in the community were irrevocably lost. If these Brahmans had not had to do hard and dirty work for a living, the speech and conduct of their lineage would have remained pure, and consistent with their social status their daughter would have been named not Damati, but Damayanti.[1]

Five miles from the road of pilgrimage to Badrinath,[2] between Karanaprayag and Rudraprayag, is Damati's in-law's house. I said "is," but I should have said "was." The marriage ceremony was performed when she was about eleven years

---

[1] Damati is a 'corruption' of Damayanti. Damayanti is a heroine of ancient Indian literature, whose story is told in the *Mahabharata*. She was a maiden so beautiful that the gods fell in love with her, but she had already fallen in love with a mortal, King Nala, and chose him in preference to a god for her husband. However, the main point of the story of Nala and Damayanti, as told in the *Mahabharata,* is to illustrate the evils of gambling. Nala wagered and lost both Damayanti and his kingdom. He finally got them back, but not before he endured many hardships.

[2] Badrinath is a shrine sacred to Hindus. It is in Uttar Pradesh on the bank of the Alaknanda River, 10,200 feet above sea level. It is a place of pilgrimage so holy that every pious Hindu hopes to visit it before he dies.

old. After the wedding, she stayed on in her parents' house for another two years. When Damati's husband, Vajdatt, like the other penniless young men of Garhwal, went to Lansdowne to enlist as a recruit, he brought his bride from her parents' house to help his elderly mother and father.

It may seem strange that the parents of a young and only son were elderly, but there was a reason for it. Before Vajdatt they had a daughter, and six years later, another daughter. The first girl died before she reached marriageable age. When the second daughter was eight years old, God presented a son to Narandatt. That is why by the time Vajdatt was old enough to enlist, his parents had crossed the Peak of the Hill of Youth, and had traveled some distance down the other side. It was a hard struggle to raise the grain. They had to fight and fondle the earth for it. With the son far away, they found his wife to be a great help.

What sort of girl was Damati? Whenever her mother-in-law called, she always answered only one way: "I'm coming, Mother." With a daughter-in-law like that, Vajdatt's mother became increasingly exhausted. Little by little, she surrendered all the housework to her. The mother-in-law said over and over again: "I don't understand why my body is falling apart."

Damati gathered fodder for the cattle, firewood and water for the kitchen, and manure for the fields—and if she had a spare moment, she massaged her mother-in-law's legs and waist. There was constant turmoil in the mother-in-law's body; sometimes she had muscle spasms, sometimes gas. She would get a toothache, or a part of her face or eyes swelled, or a lump of gas formed in her stomach. People advised her to take a puff of tobacco for this condition, but a woman, and a

Brahman woman at that . . . what would people say if she smoked? That worried her too.

Well, the ailment had to be treated, no matter what the consequences. The mother-in-law told Damati to fill the father-in-law's small coconut hukka with tobacco and to light it, but not to put water in it. Hidden in the small, dark room inside, she would smoke secretly. Damati knew this, but she never said anything.

When Damati came to her in-law's house, her figure was just beginning to curve. As her body reached its full growth and development, it took on a bloom and beauty like the juice and color which come only to fruit which has fully ripened. Loveliness came to her face and a sparkle to her eyes. When Vajdatt came home on his twenty-eight day leave the year before, it wrenched his heart to have to return. His desire for Damati was so powerful that in the cantonment his feet were always turning in the direction of his village.

Vajdatt learned to smoke cigarettes in the regiment. He would draw long and hard on the cigarette, flick off the ash with his finger, and as the smoke drifted out, he would daydream of his wife. What were those deep, long draws of smoke? They were sighs for Damati.

Vajdatt traded with the other soldiers in his company to get his vacation before his turn, that is to say, after nine months. This time when he left Lansdowne with his little flower-painted tin trunk, he brought a pair of old army boots for his father, a piece of thick cloth for a jacket for his mother, and for Damati a shining, varicolored silk sari, a pair of silver earrings, a little box for eye makeup, and other similar things. Vajdatt had his picture taken on the roadside by a Punjabi photographer who had a boxlike camera with a curtain around it. Since he could stay home for only twenty-eight days, he thought he would give his wife the picture before he returned to the cantonment. She could look at it and be reminded of him. That thought pleased him. When he thought of his wife while he was at the cantonment, he would draw hard on a cigarette. The smoke would fog his mind and he would envision himself and his wife together. In his fantasy, he was at home, holding his wife in his arms as he smoked a cigarette, and then making love to her.

Though the parents were delighted that Vajdatt was home on leave early, when the boy gave them only half the money he had brought last time, they did not see the connection between this and his early homecoming. First of all, Vajdatt had earned only nine months' pay, and second, he had spent some of it for gifts for his parents and a sari and silver earrings and other articles for Damati. Also, while associating with other soldiers, he had acquired a taste for cigarettes. Vajdatt's parents saw only that he gave them half as much money as before, and he had brought his wife an expensive sari and jewelry. They thought: "What's going on here? That wife of his is a witch. The boy is under her spell."

Furthermore, Vajdatt had learned some new habits in the cantonment. He idled the whole day away. He had no desire to do farm chores. The hands that held the rifle would not touch the plow. He would take a walk to the chatti,[3] about five miles away, buy some peanuts and candy, and when no one was around, give them to his wife. With no concern for propriety, he took his bedding to the kitchen and spread it out there. If it seemed to him that Damati was away too long at

[3] Shop and resting place on the road

her housework, he would sit there and call: "You, come here. I'm thirsty. Bring me some water." Then he would not let her leave. The parents saw all that, and though they were annoyed, they said nothing.

And there were other things they did not see. Lying back, cozy and comfortable, he would take out a cigarette and tell Damati to light it for him on the stove. Damati would give him the lighted cigarette, and he would hold her in his arms, draw on the cigarette, then put it between her lips and insist that she take a puff too. At first the smoke made Damati dizzy and she would cough. But soon she began to enjoy it. When she felt giddy, she would put her head down on Vajdatt's chest and close her eyes. Damati liked it too.

Even before Vajdatt's holiday was over, the mother-in-law's heart had turned against Damati. The moment he left, she treated Damati with increasing harshness. In irritation, the wife said: "What's gotten into the old woman? I do all the housework and she does all the criticizing." And Damati started to ignore her. When Damati was called, she seemed not to hear. The mother-in-law boiled with anger and frustration. Damati stayed as far away from her as possible. When she went out for firewood or water or fodder, she would stay away a long time. When the mother-in-law was in the house, she would go to the fields and spread manure. If mother-in-law was in the fields, she would stay in the house. And if there was no opportunity to put distance between them, Damati would go to the cowshed and lie down on the fodder which had been gathered for the winter. She no longer had any interest in housework or the farm chores.

In the beginning, the mother-in-law, partly out of affection for the bride of her only son and partly out of interest in her own convenience, had told Damati, "Everything is yours anyway. Can I take it with me when I die? You look after everything now." She gave Damati the responsibility for the entire household and the keys to both her tin boxes as well. The mother-in-law kept several pieces of silver jewelry in those boxes. When she was angry, she took everything back including the keys to the boxes, and tied them all to her waistband. Matters reached the point where she even began to dole out the flour and rice for cooking. She measured them out so that there would not be enough left to satisfy Damati's hunger after the parents had eaten. The mother-in-law, in jealousy, nagged at her and thought: "That witch has turned my son's heart against me . . . he gave her all his savings . . . she has hidden his money away, and now I have to feed her."

When Damati washed her hair, the earrings from Vajdatt would get entangled in the strands. One day she removed them before washing her hair and placed them on the shelf in the little inside room. On returning, she could not find them anywhere. When she asked her mother-in-law, the old woman shouted: "Look at the witch! She hides her jewelry and then calls me a thief!" Damati wiped away her tears in silence. Then one day her little box of eye makeup disappeared too.

When Vajdatt left for the cantonment, he gave Damati his photograph. She kept it in a cigarette box together with one cigarette she had saved. Fearing her mother-in-law might steal that too, Damati hid the cigarette in the thatch of the cowshed. As the mother-in-law increased her abuse of Damati, she also decreased the quantity of food, to the point where Damati was going hungry. One day after the mother-in-law had doled out an even smaller amount of flour than usual for the meal and was going outside, Damati took three extra handfuls from the bin and put them on the kneading board. The mother-in-law turned around and saw her.

Loud enough for all the neighbors to hear, she shrieked at Damati: "Thief! Look at the huge belly on that witch! You no-good—!"

The mother-in-law exploded with anger and rambled on abusively. Damati dropped the kneading board in anger and left the kitchen. She wanted to cry her heart out. She went to the cowshed and lay down and wept for a long time. She was getting hungry, and she thought: "Who knows when he will come? By the time he comes, that mother-in-law will starve me to death."

The mother-in-law baked the bread for dinner and called her husband in to eat. Later, the sound of banging pots told Damati that the mother-in-law was angrily cleaning the pots herself in the backyard. Damati felt pangs of hunger. She saw the cigarette tin hidden in the thatch, and thought: "I'll have a smoke." She took a cigarette and tiptoed to the kitchen to light it.

Damati had slipped into the kitchen very quietly, but the mother-in-law heard her, and said to herself: "First that wretch thinks she'll frighten me by being sullen, and now she comes to steal." She put the pots down and quietly stole into the kitchen to catch Damati in the act. She muttered: "I'll grab that witch and set her hair on fire." She peeped into the kitchen and saw Damati sitting in front of the stove lighting a cigarette.

The mother-in-law's eyes widened. She stared, open-mouthed, as though a stone had dropped from the sky. When she collected herself, she started to scream: "Look at that wretch! . . . Smoking cigarettes! . . . What a whore she is!

So that's how she put a spell on my boy! She steals money and goes to the chatti to buy cigarettes. Oh, God, that woman will seduce all the boys around here!" She went out into the courtyard her arms flailing, calling to the neighbors to listen.

Father-in-law had finished his dinner and was relaxing, reclining against the wall as he smoked his hukka. He got up, came into the kitchen and shouted: "Bastard, get out of this house! How did a whore from the bazaar get into a Brahman's house? Get out this minute or I'll cut off your head!"

It was noon and the neighbors had all come in from the fields at meal time. Hearing the excitement at Vajdatt's house, they all gathered there. The women stood astonished, covering their lips with the edge of their scarves. The old man and the women all chimed in together: "Is this the wife of a Brahman? This is a prostitute! She will contaminate everybody's caste. Who will take water from this house?"

Terrified, Damati threw the cigarette into the stove, and cowered in a corner of the kitchen. The mother-in-law then seized her by the hair and dragged her to the courtyard Damati was driven like a helpless goat pulled by its ear. In front of everybody, the mother-in-law kicked her and yelled: "Get out, whore! Leave my house!" The father-in-law, concerned about his pipe going out, puffed away at his hukka while at the same time swearing at Damati and threatening to behead her if she didn't leave the house.

Damati, beaten and cast out, her clothes all torn, hid her face in her scarf and ran into the fields. She stopped under a *tun* [4] tree and stood and wondered: "What shall I do? Where shall I go?" Certainly not to her in-laws' house. There was

---

[4] A tree with yellow flowers; *cedrela toona*

only one road for her to follow in all the world—the road that
led to the cantonment to tell her husband how unjustly she
had been treated by his parents. She started walking quickly
toward the chatti.

Damati reached Rudraprayag in the late afternoon. She
stopped at the shops and asked directions to the cantonment.
A young girl about sixteen, alone and perplexed, asking the
way to the cantonment—when Hiraman, the shopkeeper of
the chatti saw this, it didn't take him long to assess the
situation. He spoke reassuringly to Damati and urged her to
sit down and tell him why she left home so distressed and
why she wanted to go to the cantonment. Weeping and
wiping her eyes with her scarf, Damati told the whole story of
how shabbily she had been treated by her in-laws, and how,
tormented by hunger, she had smoked a cigarette. And she
finished her story saying: "My husband is in the cantonment.
I am going to him." Hiraman criticized the mother-in-law and
soothed Damati saying: "Of course, of course. Whom does a
woman have but her husband? You must go to him. But you
are completely exhausted. You are a Brahman's daughter.
Have something to eat and rest awhile. I will show you the
way. Go inside now and rest. Look upon this house as your
own." He gave Damati some nuts and sweets and a pitcher of
water, saying: "We are Brahmans too. You can drink water
from our pitcher. Don't worry."

Hiraman took her to a little room inside so that she could
not be seen by any passerby on the road. Damati was anxious
to start out for the cantonment. After an hour had passed, she
said: "I'm going now. Just show me the way."

"Oh, how can I do that?" Hiraman chided her affectionately: "I can't let you go away hungry. A daughter of my

neighbor is the same as my own. Here, cook some rice and eat. It is a two-hundred-mile journey. Be patient. I will put you in the care of some people who are traveling that way. You are only a helpless woman. You don't know your way around here. How can you go alone?" Hiraman gave Damati dal, rice and cooking utensils. While she was cooking, it got dark. She was impatient to start out for the cantonment, but it had been a long time since she had eaten her fill or had spoken to a sympathetic person. She started dozing and lay down on the floor and fell asleep.

Something touched her shoulder and awakened her. In a corner of the room, a small lamp cast a faint glow. Hiraman's hand was on Damati's shoulder, and he was smiling and asked: "Are you going to go on sleeping?" Damati moved beyond his reach and rubbed her sleepy eyes. Seeing her move away, Hiraman sat down on the floor, took out a tin of cigarettes and offered them, saying: "Here take one. At least have a cigarette." Damati shook her head and continued rubbing her eyes.

"You know how to smoke. Have one," Hiraman urged.

"Uh, uh," Damati shook her head again: "When did I smoke? Only when my husband gave me . . . One cigarette and see what happened to me. Now I'm going to the cantonment."

"Why are you rushing to the cantonment?," Hiraman asked, edging closer to her, "What do you think will happen when you get there? He will beat you even more for having left home. He will tell you that you have made him lose face before the world." Rubbing her shoulder, he said: "Have some fun . . . Why not?"

"Stop!" Damati said, standing up and moving away.

"All right. If that's the way you feel about it," Hiraman said, smiling, "you can leave before dawn. No one goes on the road in the middle of the night. The soldiers patrol the roads at night, and if they see anyone they consider him a thief and arrest him. Some travelers will be going that way before daybreak, and I will put you in their care. Just sit down."

Damati refused to sit down near him. When Hiraman tried to persuade her to she said: "How can I sit near a strange man?" And she continued to stand at a distance.

Hiraman thought for a moment and said: "All right. Since I embarrass you, you sleep here. I'm leaving. Some travelers are going to the cantonment in the morning. I'll go now and tell them to take you with them."

Hiraman left by the back door. Damati lay down on the floor again and started thinking about the cantonment. She felt uneasy about going to a strange place, but how could she go back to the house? After awhile she fell asleep again. At midnight, Hiraman woke her and said: "A friend of mine who is going there is waiting outside. He's a very nice man. You must be careful, understand? Women who travel alone on the road are suspected by the police of being runaways, and are arrested. So, if anyone asks you, just say you are his wife."

This displeased Damati. "Don't say that!," she said: "How can I say that another man is my husband?"

"You are a fool," Hiraman spoke coolly, like a man of experience, "Is someone making you someone else's wife? You are a village girl. What do you know about traveling on the road? What I am telling you is for your own good. The government has ordered that no woman can travel on the road alone. If anyone asks your name or where you're from, just

say that your name is Nanda, that you are with your husband
and that he will answer any questions. When a woman goes
with a man who isn't her husband, the police arrest her and
take her to the police station. They will beat you and rape
you. This man is a Brahman and a gentleman. Look upon
him as your own brother."

Hiraman led Damati out of the shop onto the dark road and
told the man who was waiting there: "This is one of our own
girls, brother. Make the proper inquiries at the cantonment
and hand her over to her husband. I don't want her to have
any difficulties on the way. And bear this in mind—a Brahman's daughter has the same status as a cow. Do you understand?"

Damati walked along with the man in the dark. After a
short distance he said: "How do you happen to be on the road
in the dark?" He spoke with a strange accent. Damati again
recounted simply and truthfully the details of the outrageous
way she had been treated by her in-laws, how they beat her
and turned her out when she smoked a cigarette, and how she
was now going to her husband in the cantonment. This man
too, to comfort her, condemned her in-laws. He said: "How
could they do such a despicable thing to a good girl like you?
You should have milk and sweets to eat and jewelry and fine
clothes to wear. You shouldn't be carrying cow dung and
weeding fields at your age. Oh, God, look at your skirt and
scarf. When we get to Srinagar,[5] I'll get you a sari in the
bazaar."

Damati was moved by his sympathy, but she said, "Why

[5] This is not the famous Srinagar of Kashmir, but Srinagar in Uttar
Pradesh eighteen miles from Rudraprayag, a small town on the road of
pilgrimage to Badrinath.

should you? What do I need a sari for now? My husband will get me one. He brought me a beautiful silk sari, but my mother-in-law snatched it away from me."

They camped out one night and arrived in Srinagar the next evening. The man took Damati through the bazaar to a narrow street into a rather large house. Damati had never seen such a big house or one like it. The courtyard was enclosed by walls, and there were doors in the walls. Damati was exhausted by the long journey on foot. She sat down against the wall.

The man went out and returned immediately, bringing a young boy with him. "He will bring you water for washing," he told Damati, "and I will go to the bazaar for rice and dal." Damati sat while the boy brought one pitcherful and then another. Then he brought some firewood. In the meantime, the man came back. He had made a bundle of rice, dal, salt and spices in his kerchief, and had brought some ghee in a small leaf cup. Also, wrapped in paper, was a new print sari. He said: "After you wash, put on this new sari and cook your dinner."

Damati washed, then went into the kitchen the man had shown her and cooked the rice and dal. She put his food on a platter and she ate too. Then she lay down on a mat. The man ate and went out. When he returned, he bolted the courtyard door and sat down on the mat near Damati. Damati jumped up, and the man, to detain her, put his hand on her body, saying, "Don't be upset. Listen. Here—take a cigarette."

Damati said, "Stop!" She pushed his hand away and got away from him. He snatched her hand, laughing, and said teasingly: "Oh come on, have a cigarette. You smoke, don't you?"

Damati pulled her hand free and moved away to the other wall. "I don't smoke . . . I only smoked one cigarette, and that was because my husband gave it to me," she said angrily.

The man stood in front of her blocking her way, and flung at her furiously: "You ——! How long have I been feeding you for nothing? Take off my sari!" Damati wasn't frightened. She said proudly: "First return my clothes, and I'll throw your sari at you. Did I ask you for it?"

The man didn't intend to be put down in this way by a wilful woman. He swore, rushed at her and began pulling off her sari. Struggling for her clothes, Damati held tightly to the sari. As the man tore it from her, she pinched, bit and elbowed him, but it was all futile. When more than half the sari was in the man's hands, Damati started to cry and beg for mercy, but he paid no attention. He was going to teach that unmanageable woman a lesson! He finished pulling the sari off her, reviling her all the while, while Damati cowered and shrank with shame. He left the room, looked in from the outside and went away. Damati sank to the floor, weeping.

In the pitch darkness of the room, she did not know whether it was day or night. Exhausted by weeping, she berated herself: "Why did I come to this strange place knowing nothing? Better to have died there. Why did I smoke that cigarette?" Her body sagged with fatigue. When she could no longer sit up, she collapsed against the wall and fell asleep.

When she awoke, there were shafts of light from the gaps in the door. As she lay there, she again reproached herself for her blunder. Then she dozed off. She woke up to see rays of

sunlight beaming broader and brighter through the gaps in
the door, but the door itself had not been opened. She fixed
her eyes on the streaks of light on the mud floor and she wept
a little and she sobbed a little. She was thirsty. She needed to
go to the toilet outside. She got up and banged and slammed
at the door. With all her strength she pulled and dragged at
it, but it did not open. She knew she would die here like this.
And she wept. But what could her tears accomplish?

She lay there lifeless. She wanted to hang herself, but she
had nothing to hang herself with. She remembered when she
was standing under the tree, planning to go to the cantonment. "Why didn't I hang myself then?" she thought. She
watched the rays of light through the chinks in the door grow
fainter and fainter, and again she was in total darkness. Spent
and hopeless, she no longer even sobbed—she waited only to
die. She became dizzy, feeling thirst and the need to relieve
herself. Visions of the village and the road whirled before her
eyes in the dark room.

Light came through the chinks of the door again, but
Damati was not aware of it. She was only partly conscious.
Hearing the sound of the door being opened, she managed
with great effort to sit up, in a huddled position. The man
came in. He tossed Damati's clothes at her and said: "Get up
and wash yourself." He left, leaving the door of the room
open, but locking the courtyard door from the outside.

By the time he returned an hour and a half later, Damati
had drunk some water, relieved herself, taken a bath, put on
her old clothes, and was sitting propped against the wall,
leaning her chin on her hands. She felt a little better. The
man had brought something wrapped in his kerchief and a

pitcher of milk. He put the kerchief in front of her and said: "Take it. I've brought puris and vegetables for you. Have something to eat and drink the milk."

"I don't want anything," Damati pleaded, with joined hands. "Just let me go."

"Oh, how can you go on an empty stomach? What did I say to you? You get excited too easily." And he explained: "The shopkeeper told me to take you to the cantonment, and that I will do. So have something to eat. If you go alone, you will get lost. If you were to fall into the hands of the police, do you know what would happen? You really don't know anything. I will take you there, but first eat something."

Damati was very hungry. The food was right in front of her and she began to eat. The man left again, locking the door of the courtyard, but leaving the room door open. When he returned, he sat at some distance from Damati and spoke persuasively: "Look, don't be a fool. When a woman leaves her house, there is no place for her in that household anymore. A woman of a Brahman household is like a clay pot. Once there's a crack in it, it is worthless. Your husband might even cut off your head. If you were to go to the village, what would you do there? Carry dung and firewood on your head? Come with me to the plains. You will have fine jewelry and clothes to wear and cream and sweets to eat."

Damati joined her hands and begged, "No. Have pity on me. Just let me go. I'll go my own way, maybe to the cantonment or back to the village."

"Now you are angry with me," the man said in a conciliatory tone: "All right, don't come with me. There's another Brahman; he's from your district. He's going to the cantonment this evening and you can go along with him. Is that all right? I'll speak to him." He got up and went out, and again Damati heard the door being bolted from the outside.

Damati was frightened. God knows what kind of man this one would be.

She tried all the courtyard doors, but found them locked. She inspected the whole area. The courtyard wall was higher than her head. Even when she raised her arms, she could not reach the top of the wall. The wall of the toilet in the corner of the courtyard was the same height as she. There were holes in the back wall, but they were very small. She would do anything to escape, but the holes were too small. Then she had an idea! There was a pitcher near the toilet wall. She turned it upside down, stood on it, and climbed onto the low wall. From there, she climbed over the courtyard wall and jumped outside.

Once in the street, she walked very quickly and after a very few steps, arrived at a bazaar. She began asking people the way to the cantonment.

Seeing a woman in torn clothes, all alone, confused, and asking the way to the cantonment, people gathered round. The police were also attracted when they saw the growing crowd. Damati was taken to the police station. The daroga asked her name, village and reason for coming to Srinagar. Damati told her whole story again, honestly and fully, how her smoking a cigarette caused her to be beaten and thrown out. With a slight smile the daroga said: "Then you do smoke? Here, take one." And he offered her a cigarette.

"Oh no," Damati objected, "I smoked only because my husband offered me a cigarette."

Then a search was begun for the man who had brought

Damati to Srinagar and for the house where he had imprisoned her. The police took her to the bazaar and into several different streets, but she could identify nothing. She kept insisting: "I came here by myself. I am going to the cantonment."

A woman who had run away from home could not be permitted to go where she pleased. However, it was against regulations to hold her overnight at the police station. She should have been taken immediately to the jail at Pauri in the custody of a guard, but there was no one around at the time and night was approaching. The policemen took her to several houses to find the scoundrel who had brought her here from Rudraprayag. They repeatedly offered her sweets and cigarettes in an intimate way. Damati turned her face away in anger. She was prepared to struggle against them, if necessary. The next day two policemen took Damati to Pauri.

When she was brought before the magistrate, she told her entire story again truthfully. She told him she had no intention of returning to that house—she wanted to go to her husband in the cantonment. It was explained to her that she would not be allowed to go off just like that. She would never find her husband. The government would send for Vajdatt and she would be placed in his care. But until then she would have to stay in jail.

Damati did not know Vajdatt's serial number and the number of his company, so it took a little time to find Vajdatt of Kanar Village in Jyola Patti. Meanwhile, Vajdatt's father had sent him two postcards with a complete report: His wife had become loose and incorrigible. She had stolen money from the house and spent it at the chatti for cigarettes. She had also stolen jewelry and sold it. Damati was a symbol of shame to the entire neighborhood. Finally, she had run away with a man she met on the road. In the letter the elderly father reassured the young son: "Don't give it a thought. Who needs a wife like that? We have started talking to some people, and when you come home on leave, a wedding will be arranged for you."

When Vajdatt received the summons to appear in court in Pauri to identify his wife and take custody of her, he believed everything his father had written.

In Rudraprayag, Hiraman told Pandit Manahar that there was a very young, ignorant Brahman girl in his shop who had run away from home because her in-laws had been giving her trouble. Manahar bought Damati from Hiraman for 80 rupees. He planned to keep the girl in Srinagar for about a month. He would amuse himself with her for awhile and she would learn more sophisticated ways. Then he would take her to the plains and sell her for about 500 rupees. Manahar had handled a number of women this way. When he was beaten down by Damati's resistance in Srinagar, he realized his mistake. He had been too hasty. The slut was annoyed with him. Now it would be difficult to control her. He saw no purpose in wasting his time with this encumbrance, and decided to turn her over to Shivdatt right here in Srinagar for about 150 rupees.

He brought Damati her clothes and some food to calm her while he went out to look for Shivdatt. He didn't find Shivdatt at home and he started back. In the bazaar he heard that the police had picked up a runaway woman asking the way to the cantonment and had taken her to the police station. His suspicion was aroused. When he got home, Damati had disappeared. Then he saw the upended pitcher and realized how she had jumped over the wall and that it was she who was now in the hands of the police.

Manahar had no intention of throwing away his 80 rupees. He wasn't concerned about the police. If he had to, he could deal with them. All his anger was directed against Hiraman. That bitch is an accomplished liar, he thought. She will fool the police and go back to Hiraman, and he will sell her again. That is why that lying swindler sold her so cheap. Furious, Manahar came to a decision: "All right, son. Cheating among us? I'll teach you a lesson you'll remember for a long time. Now let me see where that woman goes."

He was an experienced man, and the thought had occurred to him when Damati resisted him with such force that perhaps she was not a loose woman. If she were, why would she put up such a fight? He decided that he would wait and see whether she returned to Hiraman or to her own man.

When Manahar learned that Damati had been set to Pauri, he went there too. He was in court when Vajdatt and Damati were brought before the magistrate. Manahar was a little surprised that they recognized each other. He waited patiently to see how the matter would end. Vajdatt acknowledged the fact that Damati was his wife, but when the court placed her in his care, he refused to accept her. He said that he would not take back an immoral woman who had run away from home. Hearing this, Damati gasped and stared at him. Her head sagged and she closed her eyes. When she looked up again, Vajdatt had gone.

Now the government was not willing to let Damati have space in jail. It was the responsibility of the government to deliver the runaway wife to Vajdatt since she was his property. However, when Vajdatt refused to exercise his right to his wife, the government was no longer concerned with her.

The magistrate pitied Damati and explained to her that she could request support from her husband if she wished. Damati shook her head. Then he rendered his decision: "You can go wherever you like now." The world grew dark before Damati's eyes, but she had to leave the courtroom.

Pandit Manahar sat watching the entire chapter to its end. Damati, trembling, her eyes as expressionless as the dead, left the courtroom. Where would she go now?

"Say, where were you?" a voice behind her said. She turned around and saw Manahar and was silent.

Manahar said comfortingly: "There was no reason to be angry. I didn't mean to bother you. I came here looking all over for you. I told you that there was no place for you in your house. Don't be distressed. Come. My house is yours."

Damati thought for a moment, then walked along with him. Manahar took her into a house on a street in the bazaar and respectfully offered her a mat to sit on. Damati sat down silently, looking down at the floor, her back against the wall.

"You must be very tired. Here, smoke a cigarette. It will relax you," Manahar said, as he took out a tin of cigarettes and offered them to Damati. Damati, still looking down, took one. Tears flowed from her eyes.

PURCHASED HAPPINESS

Yashpal again uses North India hill country as the setting for, "Purchased Happiness" (Parāyā Sukh). The story begins in Pathankot, ends in Dalhousie, fifty miles away, and concerns the events which take place en route. Yashpal's gift for description makes the bustle and confusion of Pathankot Station, the rainy ride to the dak bungalow and the refuge it offers, all come alive. His portrayal of the character of Sethi, the businessman to whom all persons are commodities and all commodities have a price, has its counterpart in many societies.

Urmila is the lovely young woman for whom Yashpal clearly feels great compassion. In many other stories he has portrayed women handicapped and disadvantaged in Indian society. However, this story does not pit Indian society against Indian womanhood. Here Urmila has a choice. This is rather a contest between a shrewd, rich businessman and a poor, beautiful, but rather naive and weak young woman. Sethi is the businessman to whom everything is purchasable—even happiness. But Urmila is so easily purchased that there is no great conquest or victory for there was not even a struggle. It could be argued that Urmila lacks the element of strength and will to resist which would have given the story greater impact. Nonetheless Sethi and Urmila are real; so is the situation. And that may be exactly what the author is trying to say.

THICK clouds so crowded the sky that it was impossible to know whether the sun had risen. Gusts of cold wind blew hard, heavy with moisture. The travellers waiting in Pathankot Station for their buses to leave for the mountains shivered, wrapping their garments tighter about them. The bus drivers, in the meantime, darted about, rounding up passengers. They were even more eager than the travellers to get on with the journey.

Outside, the long railway platform was deserted except for an occasional coolie. Mr. Sethi, warm in a heavy suit and overcoat, strolled along the stone paving at the side of the platform. The cold mountain wind could not pierce his clothes. It only caressed his face and ruffled his hair. The chill of the wind which was drawing the very life out of the hundreds of other travellers, simply exhilirated Sethi. For him it was a moment of tranquility, and his thoughts turned inward.

While the bus drivers gathered their passengers together in the Third Class Waiting Room, the taxi drivers were glancing timidly through the screens of the First Class Waiting Room, attempting to estimate their prospects for passengers. One driver approached Sethi, salaamed respectfully and said, "Sir, I have a very comfortable car."

Sethi did not answer, but continued to savor the coolness of

the air. He did not want his serenity shattered with talk.
There was no need for him to look for a taxi; taxis were
always looking for him. The driver stood aside waiting for the
sahib's reply, but Sethi did not give him a thought.

Sethi saw the door of the Women's Waiting Room open. A
young woman came out wearing a long black coat over her
white sari. Clutching her finger was a small child about a year
and a half or two years old. They walked down to the other
side of the lonely platform away from Sethi. Watching them,
it seemed to him that the young woman, walking toward the
East, her finger held by the child, was the embodiment of a
fulfilled life. He felt his own existence to be futile and
aimless, like a shred of vagabond cloud tossed about in the
wind. But the life of this young woman was like a rain cloud
which first nourished the field, then spread a protective cover
over the ripening crops. The child wobbled on his little fat
legs as he hung onto the mother's finger, while her serene,
sedate and steady motion was like a cargo-laden ship floating
smoothly along the current.

Sethi leaned against a lamppost and watched the pair—
mother and child. They walked to the end of the platform
and then started back. Turning about, she withdrew her right
hand, offered the child a finger of her left hand and began to
walk towards Sethi. The boy's existence depended on the
young woman as the fruit depends on the vine. As they came
nearer, her slender, supple form, the large eyes in her fair face
glowing with health, the child's tiny nose, his big round eyes
and shining cheeks . . . all these came into sharp focus
through the thick lenses of Sethi's eyeglasses. He completely
forgot his desire for solitude in the coolness of the fresh air.

A cab driver salaamed to the lady and offered his services.

Then a bus driver spoke to her. As an experienced business-man, Sethi realized that the lady was looking for good but inexpensive transportation. The buses could not leave before seven o'clock, but a taxi could go at any time. The bus passengers were still waiting because it was too early, but the taxi drivers were waiting because the sahib-log [1] were in no hurry to leave.

Sethi had an idea. He pushed himself forward from the lamppost, straightened up and glanced toward the cab driver. The driver came running and salaamed again.

Sethi asked, "Do you have a good car?"

"Sir, I have a brand-new Austin Saloon."

"Let's go then."

"Sir, no other passenger?"

"No, we will leave immediately, but if you can make some extra money, you may take another passenger."

The driver made an even deeper bow.

Sethi's luggage was brought out of the waiting room: three suitcases, a large holdall and two small attaché cases. The driver ran up to the lady, bowed, and they settled on a nominal sum for the ride. Sethi watched all this.

The lady's few scraps of luggage appeared—only one suit-case and a holdall. Carrying the child, she followed close behind Sethi. He sat in front with the driver while she and the child sat comfortably in the back.

The car sped off, cutting through the cold air. Sethi was comforted by the presence of someone behind him. Although he had paid for the use of the entire car, he did not mind

---

[1] Sahib-log refers to the upper classes. In this case the expression is used to distinguish between those who could afford a taxi and occupy the First Class Waiting Room and the other less affluent travellers.

sitting in the narrow front seat. The child, watching the houses and the trees along the road speed by, kept jumping up and down, clutching the seat in front of him. Bouncing about in his excitement, he would sometimes knock off Sethi's hat and sometimes his head would bump against Sethi's arm.

His constant jumping embarrassed his mother. Several times she told the boy to quiet down and scolded him gently, but both Sethi and she ended up laughing at him. Then he tried to climb into the front seat. Sethi turned around, picked him up and sat him in his lap. Sethi's heart throbbed with a strange emotion at the touch of the chubby, robust, soft body of the child. This was a new sensation for him. Sethi, who had fought and struggled every inch of the way to achieve success, suddenly realized the total failure and pointlessness of his life. Staring at the child's face intensified his realization of the emptiness of his own existence.

As the car sped along and the landscape flew past, he saw again all his past life like the unfolding sequence of a movie film. When his father died, he had to drop out of high school and move from place to place to try to make a living. Finally he found a job working for a contractor from morning till night at backbreaking labor for 20 rupees a month. He began to subcontract one job after another . . . then he became a contractor himself. He had dug and scratched and pushed for each rupee until money began to drop into his hands by the thousands and the lakhs.[2] He had just made a profit of two and a half lakhs on a railway bridge contract.

Sethi had valued only one thing in his life—money. He worked day and night to make more. Now he owned stock in

[2] A lakh is 100,000. In this context it refers to lakhs of rupees.

large companies and he was a millionaire. What could he not command by merely scrawling his name on a tiny piece of paper—an Imperial Bank checkbook tucked away in his pocket? But in all this time what had he gained aside from money? On the other hand, what couldn't he have with money?

Hundreds of Sethi's relatives, whom he did not even care to acknowledge, much less to know, identified themselves using his name. Their hearts brimming over with love, they wanted to be with him always. There weren't enough honors for him. Political and social organizations vied with one another to make him their patron and president. But what satisfaction did he get from all this?

How many performances of love and affection have been played for Sethi! He saw in those shy and longing girlish eyes only greed for his wealth and a plot to entrap him. And realizing this, how could he accept it? No one appealed to him. He drove them away like flies from a lump of gur.[3] His only passion was money.

Now he does not lack money; nonetheless he strives for more. His life's goal is only to increase his wealth. Money flows toward him now just as water from streams, large and small, all converge into one great river during the rainy season. Thousands of men labor in scores of companies under his direction to produce wealth, and the money flowing from these enterprises are all channeled into Sethi's account. As his wealth and income grow, he devises new channels to funnel the flow.

Sethi had no unusual expenses. He had no indulgences.

---

[3] A hard, brownish, coarse sugar. Sometimes called jaggery.

How much does it cost a single man to live? His personal expenditures were no more than 1,000 to 1,200 rupees a month. Until today the thought of happiness had never entered his mind, but suddenly in the whip of the cold wind, he was struck by a feeling of emptiness.

The child stood with his shoes on Sethi's fine coat. First he would put his hands on the ice-cold windshield and then touch his face, giggling in glee. Being trod on by the child's feet gave Sethi a sort of joy. His eyes became moist and his lip trembled. He became intensely absorbed in the child's play.

Sethi became aware of a woman behind him but close to him, one who was anxious, yet overflowing with motherly love, whose presence was pervasive as the shade offered by a tree and alluring as the flower whose seed gives life to a tree; a woman who places a steadying and protective hand on her child, who drives the arrow of desire into the heart of a man, and whose smile is a rainbow in which the seductive glance, the comfort of protection, the shelter of blessings and the fire of desire are all blended. Her magnetism drew him upward, while the child on his lap held him down. Sethi, lost in a sort of reverie, felt a strange current coursing through his body.

As the car kept climbing up the mountain road, the clouds became thicker and the air grew colder and wetter. Drops of water accumulated and trickled down the windshield. The windshield wipers were sweeping continuously in front of the driver and the baby grabbed for them. Sethi was holding his chubby arms and did not want to let them go. The child twisted around and looked at Sethi. He was fascinated by the gem-studded tieclasp in Sethi's necktie and started to pull it off. Sethi unpinned it and put it on the child's coat. As he did this, his large pink dust goggles bent over the child's face.

With half his face hidden, Sethi saw a reflection in the glass.
The mother on the seat behind him had put her finger to her
lips motioning to the child to sit still. Sethi turned around and
said on behalf of the child, "That's all right. It doesn't matter." There was a tender smile on his lips. The mother's heart
melted.

The driver slowed down and said apologetically, "Sir, it's
raining hard up ahead. The fog is very thick."

Sethi answered, "Don't worry. Just go slowly."

The rain, pouring down from the upper reaches of the
mountains, formed streams on both sides of the road. The car,
winding up the mountain, churned through the flowing
water, spraying it into the air like a fountain. Rubbing the
lamp of science and making a wish, the genie-car continued to
make its way effortlessly through the cloudy mists and spray,
carrying Sethi, the lady and the baby ever upward.

They continued on for two hours without stopping and at
the halfway point reached the dak bungalow.[4] The car, turning, entered the gate of the bungalow compound and stopped.
Because of the night-long heavy rains, there had been landslides in two places and the road ahead was closed. Travellers
were not permitted to go on. Outside the compound, a number of half-drenched people had taken shelter under the roofs
of tin and thatch. Within the compound the burdened and
rain-soaked oxen and mules watched with terrified eyes the
helter-skelter scurrying of the helpless human beings. The

[4] Dak bungalows are commonly found in tourist areas in India. They
are generally maintained by the government and usually contain eating
and sleeping facilities. The dak bungalow in the story is quite elaborate
since it contains a number of sleeping rooms and a full-time cook. This is
not surprising since Dalhousie was a famous hill station and the road
between Pathankot and Dalhousie subject to landslides.

travellers were awaiting the orders of the clouds and the Government, and the animals, in turn, were waiting for their masters' decision.

The driver opened the car door and Sethi got out. The child kept holding on to Sethi's finger, and with the lady following them, they all went into the dak bungalow. Seeing the car, the chaprassi [5] and the cook salaamed.

The uniformed cook inquired politely whether Sethi wanted breakfast. Sethi said yes. The lady had brought a bottle of milk in her basket for the child. She did not order anything. A schoolmistress earning sixty rupees a month is not accustomed to eating in a dak bungalow. She sat down in an easy chair on the veranda, and without looking at Sethi, called to the child, Ballu, to come and drink his milk. Without looking at the lady Sethi said, "Ballu will drink warm milk." The cook informed the memsahib [6] that breakfast was ready. He assumed that the gentleman, the lady and the child were all one family. The lady was aware of the cook's assumption, but this was no time to make a fuss. She said to Sethi in a gracious and refined voice in English, "Please eat your breakfast. I really don't want any."

He insisted politely, "A cup of tea will do you good in this cold."

Sethi, the lady and Ballu went inside for breakfast. To those on the other side of the walls outside the shelter, they appeared to be a small family—a husband, wife and child. The cook who went in and out of the room was the only representative and witness of that world. The lady felt it would not be proper to indicate uncertainty or anxiety in his

[5] Orderly; servant.
[6] Lady

presence since this would betray a feeling of guilt on her part. Without hesitation she started to pour tea into the cups. Sethi fed a tiny bit of omelet into Ballu's mouth. The child began to chew away at it.

The cook stood behind the lady and asked, "Sir, will you have any biscuits, jam or fruit?"

Sethi answered, "Bring them on."

All sorts of delicacies stored away in the dak bungalow were opened one after another and appeared on the table in half-opened tins and on plates. Sethi chuckled as he gave the child a bit of each to taste. Seeing the child's pleasure, the mother was delighted, but she kept asking Sethi to stop, saying, "Please, no more. He is not hungry now. It will upset his stomach."

Sethi, whose shyness had vanished because of the child, asked, "Do you live in Dalhousie?"

"Yes. My name is Mrs. Madan.[7] Mr. Madan works in the Office of Military Accounts. I am a schoolteacher. I was visiting my sister in Amritsar."

What could Sethi say to introduce himself?

He said, "How nice!" His own life seemed to him totally without foundation or form.

"Are you going to Dalhousie for the summer?" Mrs. Madan asked.

"No. Just for a couple of days on business. Dalhousie is a nice place. A very nice place. It has beautiful scenery."

"Why didn't you bring your family along?" asked Mrs. Madan.

"No . . . I have none at all . . . I am single. My name is

---

[7] The author's choice of names is symbolic. *Madan* is the god of love. A *seth* is a great merchant or moneylender.

R. L. Sethi. I am a contractor. I built the new church in Amritsar." Stirring the tea with his spoon and looking at the wall, he added, "I am all alone."

At his words, Mrs. Madan was overwhelmed with tenderness and sympathy. She thought, what a good and generous man he is!

Ballu was pulling Sethi's gold watch with its leather strap all over the table. Mrs. Madan admonished him, shaking her finger and saying, "No." Then, looking at Sethi, she laughed and said, "He is very naughty."

Sethi kept running his fingers through his hair as though the restlessness in his heart were gnawing at its roots. For all that he had made a tidy fortune, he felt like a lame man on uncertain ground. Sitting before him, watching her child, Mrs. Madan's serene, soft, glowing face, her large, bright eyes, her thick hair which he could see when the border of her sari slipped off her head, her red lips, her bare throat which peeped through the triangle made by the collar of her coat . . . all these seemed to him symbols of a life beyond his reach.

Mrs. Madan looked at Sethi and felt his gaze engulfing her. A tremor went through her body, but it was not unpleasant. Rather, she began to feel more self-assured. Putting both hands on the table and looking directly at Sethi with her sparkling eyes, she said, "How hard it is raining! How will we ever get there?"

Sethi took a gold cigarette case from his pocket, lit a cigarette, blew out the smoke and said, "If the rain doesn't stop, and if we can't get there today, what does it matter? We'll get there tomorrow."

Mrs. Madan clasped her hands together and said anxiously,

though smiling, "But I must be at school tomorrow. And your work . . . that, too, will suffer."

"Yes, the work I came for, perhaps that will not be done," and noticing the cook waiting on the veranda, he called, "Bring it here." The cook immediately presented the bill on a tray.

Without glancing in the direction of the bill, Mrs. Madan asked, "When will the driver be able to start?"

Sethi said, "When I went to school, I always hoped for a holiday or some excuse not to go, but I see that school is very dear to you."

Mrs. Madan replied, "You must have been a naughty boy. Today, too, you want to play truant from work. You want the rain to continue so that you will have an excuse to enjoy a cigarette here." And she laughed.

"Oh yes, I certainly do."

"Isn't your heart in your business?"

"I never thought about it. Now I think that I have been dragging the car of my life through the mud."

The driver came to inform them that the road was not yet open. Sethi called the police station and found out that there was no chance the road would be opened for another six hours. When he saw how upset Mrs. Madan became on hearing this, he said, "The school authorities realize that it is not within your power to repair the roads."

Mrs. Madan was tired and she went to another room to lie down. Sometimes the child would run into that room and then come out to Sethi. When Mrs. Madan left, Sethi felt that someone had snatched a dish of food from his hands for fear he would become ill from overeating . . . but he was still hungry.

For a time he lay back in the easy chair watching the clouds hovering in the sky, then he paced back and forth on the veranda, sat down, and then started pacing again. There was a new picture before his eyes. He was not pursuing money, but something else. He saw himself climbing up a steep mountain. Ahead of him was the figure of a woman. He wanted to stop her, but when he stretched out his hand to catch a corner of the sari, she climbed higher. That figure, enveloped in a gossamer cloud, was Mrs. Madan.

Sethi paced back and forth and then sat down again in the easy chair. Suddenly the newly-washed rays of the sun spread their dazzling brightness over the wet grass and trees. He thought, "My hands are tied. I cannot just get up and walk into Mrs. Madan's room. What if she is asleep? What if she is awake! If only we could sit side by side . . ." Hearing the sound of a woman's footsteps, he turned and saw Mrs. Madan standing there, both hands in her coat pockets. She said, "The sun is shining. Surely six hours have passed and we can go on. What time is it?"

Ballu had the watch now and its glass and hands were broken. The only way to find out the time was to ask the driver. Six hours had indeed passed, but the road had not yet been repaired and permission had not been granted for the vehicles to go on.

The cook appeared again, salaamed and asked, "Whall I prepare something for lunch?"

"Ask the memsahib," Sethi answered, and taking Ballu by the hand, went out into the sunshine.

Realizing how the situation appeared to the cook, Mrs. Madan experienced an uneasy sort of thrill, but in view of her behavior in the morning, how could she now give any evidence of anxiety? She said, "Whatever you can prepare quickly."

Sethi would have liked to sit next to her, but he was mindful of the embarrassment she might feel. However, they did sit together at lunch. They had to make some conversation. Sethi remarked that road breakdowns were common in the mountains. The last time he was in Dalhousie, though, he arrived in the morning, finished his work in only three hours, and returned by evening. Then he asked, "Where do you live in Dalhousie?"

Mrs. Madan gave him her address and asked, "How long are you staying?"

Sethi's work in Dalhousie was of the utmost importance, but he could stay on for one, two or three days longer. His business there concerned a contract to build a new barracks on Churail Danda Hill. He had stayed at the Hillcrest Hotel before and he planned to stay there again.

As the conversation warmed, Mrs. Madan told him about herself. Her husband earned 100 rupees a month. She herself made 60 rupees a month teaching school. She had to work. They owned a bungalow on which they had borrowed 4,500 rupees when her husband fell ill. Although it was not very profitable, they did get some income from the bungalow by renting it during the season for 200 to 250 rupees. On the other hand, they had to make a monthly payment to the moneylender of 50 to 60 rupees.

Sethi thought, what are 4,500 rupees? But what could he do?

While eating lunch, they looked on with pleasure as Ballu played. Sethi wanted to keep feeding him, but Mrs. Madan asked him not to give the boy too much.

Ballu had broken Sethi's watch. Mrs. Madan begged his forgiveness, but Sethi waved aside her apology. When they finished lunch, Mrs. Madan stood up to go inside again.

Sethi plucked up his courage and asked, "Are you going to sleep again?"

"No, but what else shall I do? Isn't there some chance we will reach our destination by evening?"

"There isn't much hope. Why are you upset? If you miss school tomorrow, you will miss one day's pay, two rupees! But if my work is not done, do you know how much I'll lose? 60,000 to 65,000 rupees!"

At her look of astonishment, Sethi burst out laughing and said, "Why don't you get your house back from the moneylender? Then you won't have to work."

"But how? It is only with the greatest difficulty we have paid back 1,000."

"That's nothing. Just get it back. I'll arrange the money. I don't want interest, and you can pay the principal at your convenience."

Mrs. Madan's eyes shone and her cheeks flushed. To compose herself, she snatched Ballu, sat him down on her lap, tore the watch out of his hands and said, "If you don't take it, he will lose it."

Ballu screwed up his face to cry and Mrs. Madan shook her finger at him, saying, "Quiet, *māmā* [8] will spank." Just by that one word, *māmā*, she established her relationship with Sethi. She told him her name was Urmila and began to tell him

---

[8] *Māmā* is a child's mother's brother. By referring to Sethi in this way, Mrs. Madan "promoted" Sethi to family status and also accepted his protection. In India, a woman's brother has the special responsibility of serving as helper and protector to his sister.

about her father's house. As they sat together, evening came
—and then night.

The moon shone in the sky. The moonbeams filtering
through the pine trees cast silver rays on them. Ballu was
asleep inside. Urmila felt that being together and alone like
this in the secluded night with the moonlight above, was not
prudent. Her body was inflamed with excitement and appre-
hension.

Outside, it was cold and a chill wind was blowing. Inside
there were many rooms, but the cook, understanding them to
be all one family, had both beds made up in the same room.
No one had instructed him otherwise, but the prospect of
sleeping in the same room with Sethi frightened Mrs. Madan.
She wondered, "How will I manage this?"

It was late at night. Sethi said, "You are getting cold. Please
go to sleep."

"And you?"

"I'm not sleepy."

Mrs. Madan knew that Sethi would stay outside all night.
Her heart melted with gratitude at his concern for her comfort. Oh, what a noble man he is!

Mrs. Madan told him he really should get married and that
she had a relative—a very well-educated girl. Sethi replied, "I
have lived this way for forty-eight years, and I'll go on this
way. Marriage is like a throw of the dice. They can fall either
way." And once again, he told Urmila to go inside and get
some sleep. Urmila replied, "The moonlight is lovely, and it's
not too cold."

Together they stayed on the veranda. Sometimes Sethi
spoke and Urmila listened, and sometimes Urmila spoke and
Sethi listened.

The ninth-day moon was hidden behind the mountains. There was no way to tell the time, but more than half the night had gone. They were both shivering with cold. Urmila could not bear the thought of Sethi's catching cold because of her . . . suppose he were to fall ill? She stood up, saying, "Come, let's go inside. Don't sister and brother sleep in one room?"

As they went inside together, Sethi put his hand on Urmila's back. Wrapping themselves in blankets, they slipped into their respective beds.

The road to Dalhousie was opened early in the morning, but Sethi and Urmila decided they would wait for their tea before starting out.

Sethi asked, "Did you sleep well?" and laughed.

Urmila said, smiling, "I hope you did."

Each knew that the other had not slept a wink, but despite a sleepless night both were full of energy.

Sethi said, "I don't want to leave this bungalow." Urmila looked at him tenderly, then dropped her gaze. There were no words. Although she had a husband, she had never before known such generosity, self-discipline and affection. Every fibre of her body wanted to cry out, "You are noble! You are great!" But she couldn't utter a word.

A woman is always the loser. When she is seduced, she has lost. But when she accepts protection, then, too, she has lost.

Just before they left Sethi said, "If you have no objection, I would like to take a picture of you in this bungalow." Objection? How could Urmila have an objection? She simply looked at Sethi with gratitude. She posed for him leaning

against a pillar, tilting her head to one side, while he snapped
several pictures.

Two months are only sixty days, but what changes can be
made in that interval! Madan has left his 100-rupee-a-month
job in the Office of Military Accounts to become an Assistant
Manager of Sethi and Company at 300 rupees a month.
Urmila has quit her job as schoolmistress. Now she sits under
a large umbrella in the sunshine in front of her little bungalow, knitting a sweater for Ballu, while the dark ayah [9] from
Gond takes him for a walk.

From time to time Sethi has to come to Dalhousie. He has
the contract to build the Army barracks. There is a question
nagging at Urmila's mind—why won't Sethi consider marry-
ing her cousin? Urmila knows why, but she doesn't
want to admit it even to herself. Last time he told her quite
clearly, "It is more satisfying to inhale the fragrance of orange
than to stuff the belly with marrow.[10] As she knitted, Urmila
realized, "I am the orange."

One by one, everything Sethi had done passed before her
eyes. Sethi loved to run his fingers through her hair. Sethi
wanted her to sit next to him without his having to ask her to
do so. Sethi wanted her to wear the clothes he bought for her
when he came. She found it impossible to deny Sethi anything he desired. When he so wished, she had to wear a
blouse without sleeves or back. Of course, Urmila would wear
those very clothes anyway, and took pleasure in pleasing

[9] Nursemaid; nanny.
[10] Large, filling, tasteless vegetable.

Sethi, but her own individuality, her own will, what has happened to them?

Last Wednesday night Sethi stayed in their bungalow for half the night. What did he do? He did not put his hands out towards Urmila. He did not touch her. He sat far away, but what else did he do? He said, "I love you. I want nothing. You are my heart's desire. I just want to look at you."

Urmila could not bear it. She began to cry.

Sethi said, "Forgive me," and slipped away silently.

Urmila's eyes were fixed on the seams she was knitting in the bright light, but her mind's eye saw all the events of the other night. She was troubled by her ingratitude. That man who, without making her feel any burden of obligation, had offered her as a gift the fruits of his lifelong labor, and had never asked a thing for himself . . . whatever it might be . . . to disappoint him. . . .

Sethi told her he planned to leave his entire fortune to Ballu, so long as no one else shared it. In the plainest of terms this meant that, by fastening a padlock on Urmila's womb, Sethi was establishing his possession, whether he touched her or not. Ballu was his, Madan was his, and most of all, Urmila was his!

How self-disciplined, how noble, how great-hearted Sethi is! See how he has given away everything! Urmila has given Sethi nothing at all. She had neither the opportunity nor even the courage to give. Sethi has established his dominion over everything. How easy it was! As if he carried in his pocket the one key to all things. There was no way out of this net for Urmila, for Ballu or even for Madan—it was as though they all had been sold to him.

Urmila asked herself, "What if Sethi returns tomorrow, despondent, and repeats all this? What if he says he loves me. Will I say no again?" Then she thought, "Does it really matter?" Her heart wanted to say no to him, but did she have the right to refuse? That right which every woman has, she did not. Her very conscience denied it to her. How was her existence different from that of a prostitute? Tears began to stream down her face.

Urmila began to think back to two months ago when they had just two tiny rooms, and she would return from school exhausted, to have to endure the irritations of a stupid servant. They did not have the bare necessities . . . but she could say yes and no . . . she could do what she chose.

She wondered once again, "Will Sethi come today?" Her eyes filled with tears as she looked toward the gate. Now she no longer felt any conflict . . . only helplessness.

STORY SOURCES

All the short stories in this collection were written in Hindi by Yashpal and published by Viplav Karyalay in Lucknow. Listed below in the order they appear are: the title in English, the original title in Hindi, the title of the book in which they appeared, the date of publication of that edition, and the story pages in the book.

"Two Desperate Souls" (Dukhī-Dukhī), *Pinjre kī Uṛān*, 1957, pages 66–70

"The Book of Experience" (Anubhav kī Pustak) *Citr kā Shīrṣak*, 1955, pages 74–77

"A Name for the Painting" (Citr kā Shīrṣak), *Citr kā Shīrṣak*, 1955, pages 9–16

"Sāg" (Sāg), *Bhasmāvṛt Cingārī*, 1946, pages 102–105

"The Essence of Love" (Prem kā Sār), *Pinjre kī Uṛān*, 1957, pages 48–55

"To Uphold Righteousness" (Dharm Rakṣā), *Phulo kā Kurtā*, 1959, pages 82–96

"The Emperor's Justice" (Shahanshāh kā Nyāy), *Citr kā Shīrṣak*, 1955, pages 40–44

"One Cigarette" (Ek Cigret), *Citr kā Shīrṣak*, 1955, pages 50–67

"Purchased Happiness" (Parāyā Sukh), *Gyāndān*, 1959, pages 51–66

BIBLIOGRAPHY

Hindi

Yashpal, *Bhasmāvṛt Cingārī*, Lucknow: Viplav Karyalay, 1946
———, *Citr kā Shīrṣak*, Lucknow: Viplav Karyalay, 1955
———, *Gyāndān*, Lucknow: Viplav Karyalay, 1959
———, *Phūlo kā Kurtā*, Lucknow: Viplav Karyalay, 1959
———, *Pinjre kī Uṛān*, Lucknow: Viplav Karyalay, 1957
———, *Sinhāvalokan*, Vol. 1, Lucknow: Viplav Karyalay, Fourth Edition, 1964
———, *Sinhāvalokan*, Vol. 3, Lucknow: Viplav Karyalay, Second Edition, 1961
R. C. Pathak, Editor, *Bhargava's Standard Illustrated Dictionary of the Hindi Language*, Varanasi: Bhargava Bhushan Press, July, 1961

English

A. L. Basham, *The Wonder that was India*, New York: Grove Press, Inc., 1954
Gerald D. Berreman, *Hindus of the Himalayas*, Berkeley: University of California Press, 1963
Wm. Theodore de Bary, Editor, *Sources of Indian Tradition*, New York: Columbia University Press, Fourth Printing, 1964

S. M. Edwardes and H. L. O. Garrett, *Mughal Rule in India,* London: Oxford University Press, 1930

Ainslie T. Embree, Editor, *The Hindu Tradition,* New York: The Modern Library, 1966

Ralph T. H. Griffith, *The Hymns of the Ṛgveda,* Vol. II, Chowkhamba Sanskrit Studies, Vol. XXXV, Chowkhamba Sanskrit Series Office, Varanasi, 1963

F. S. Growse, *The Rāmāyaṇa of Tulsī Dās,* Allahabad: North-Western Provinces and Oudh Government Press, 1883

Charles H. Heimsath, *Indian Nationalism and Hindu Social Reform,* Princeton: Princeton University Press, 1964

W. Douglas Hill, *The Holy Lake of the Acts of Rama,* London: Geoffrey Cumberlege, 1952

Kabir. *Songs of Kabir,* translated by Rabindranath Tagore, New York: Macmillan, 1915

Stanley Lane–Poole, *Medieval India Under Mohammedan Rule* (A.D. 712–1764), Delhi: Universal Book & Stationery Co., 1963

V. D. Mahajan, *The Muslim Rule in India,* Delhi: S. Chand & Co., 1962

R. C. Majumdar, *History of the Freedom Movement in India,* Volumes 2 and 3, Calcutta: Firma K. L. Mukhopadhyay, 1963

R. C. Majumdar, *Three Phases of India's Struggle for Freedom,* Bombay: Bharatiya Vidya Bhavan, 1961

Kenneth W. Morgan, Editor, *The Religion of the Hindus,* New York: The Ronald Press Company, 1953

F. Max Müller, "The Upanishads," *Sacred Books of the East,* Vol. XV, Part II, Oxford: Clarendon Press, 1884

F. Max Müller, Editor, "Hymns of the Atharva-Veda," translated by M. Bloomfield, *Sacred Books of the East,* Vol. XLII, Delhi: Motilal Banarsidass, 1964

F. Max Müller, Editor, "The Grihya-Sūtras" (Rules of Vedic Domestic Ceremonies), Translated by Hermann Oldenberg,

Sacred Books of the East, Vol. XXX, Part II, Delhi: Motilal Banarsidass, 1964

A. B. Pandey, *Later Medieval India,* Allahabad: Central Book Depot, 1963

M. S. Randhawa, *Flowering Trees in India,* New Delhi: Indian Council of Agricultural Research, 1957

Gulab Singh, *Under the Shadow of Gallows,* Delhi: Roop Chand, 1963

B. Pattabhi Sitaramayya, *The History of the Indian National Congress,* Volume 1 (1885–1935), Bombay: Padma Publications, 1946

O. H. K. Spate, *India & Pakistan: A General and Regional Geography,* London: Methuen & Co., Ltd., 1963

Robert Oscar Swan, *Premchand: A Critical Evaluation of Three Stages in the Evolution of one of the Foremost Hindi Short Story Writers,* Ph.D. dissertation, University of Pennsylvania, Philadelphia, 1966

Gopal Thakur, *Bhagat Singh: The Man and His Ideas,* New Delhi: People's Publishing House, 1962

H. G. Walton, Editor, "Almora", *District Gazetteer of the United Provinces,* Vol. XXXV, Allahabad: Government Press, U.P., 1928